Brand Positioning With Power

Brand Positioning With Power

Maximize Your Marketing Impact

Robert S. Gordon

BEP

BUSINESS EXPERT PRESS

Leader in applied, concise business books

Brand Positioning With Power: Maximize Your Marketing Impact

First published in 2023 by
Business Expert Press, LLC
222 East 46th Street, New York, NY 10017
www.businessexpertpress.com

ISBN-13: 978-1-63742-551-0 (paperback)
ISBN-13: 978-1-63742-552-7 (e-book)

Business Expert Press Marketing Collection

First edition: 2023

10 9 8 7 6 5 4 3 2 1

Dedicated to my loving wife and best friend, Judy Tomlinson

Description

Powerful Brand Positioning Harnesses
Key Building Blocks

Brand Positioning With Power: Maximize Your Marketing Impact is a new take on Al Ries and Jack Trout's original positioning concept. The book **delivers measurable results** because it:

- Is remarkably easy to use;
- Presents a proven, systematic positioning process;
- Leverages exciting, practical real-world examples.

You'll see how the **three essential building blocks of positioning lead organically to increased success**, whether you are a sole proprietor or a Fortune 500 organization.

Written in a concise and conversational style, *Brand Positioning With Power* offers ground-breaking insights, including the vital role emotion plays in effective positioning. **This is the tool you need today** to take your brand from where you are to where you want to go.

Key words

brand positioning; marketing position; differentiation in business strategy; creating emotional connection with customers; market segmentation; target audience; benefit ladder; branding methods; customer loyalty; demographic analysis; strategic marketing; consumer advertising; selling strategies; business insights; psychographics

Contents

Testimonials

"Whether you are an experienced marketer or a novice, Robert Gordon's Brand Positioning With Power: Maximize Your Marketing Impact *is a must read. Gordon delivers a contemporary and meaningful guide to how positioning can act as a business's 'North Star.' He expertly provides a comprehensive framework for applying his concepts and shows, in detail, why positioning is one of the most important elements of the marketing and branding process."*—**Barry Silverman, PhD (candidate), Brand Marketer and Adjunct Professor, Branding and Integrated Communications Program, City College of New York**

"In Brand Positioning With Power: Maximize Your Marketing Impact, *Robert Gordon explains, step-by-step, why it's so important to position your brand. And he tells you how to do it! Other books tell you the why but not the how. Gordon gets right to the point, using a conversational style. He gives real-world examples showing both the steps in the process and what the outcome should be. Countless companies need to use what he is laying out here to better market their services."*—**Tim Brown, Data Management Executive**

Preface and Acknowledgments

Ask the experts who were the greatest business thinkers of all time, and people like Adam Smith, Estee Lauder, Sakichi Toyoda, Henry Ford, Steve Jobs, John D. Rockefeller, and Walt Disney repeatedly rise to the top. However, if you ask the same question about marketing—or, more specifically, about market positioning—people in the know will probably start with two names: Al Ries and Jack Trout.

Some say that Ries and Trout are the world's most innovative marketing strategists.

I, of course, completely agree. After all, this book could not exist without their insightful, groundbreaking work. I owe them a huge debt of gratitude.

My intention is to stand on their shoulders as far as I am able and provide a practical guide and handbook that marketers can use whenever they engage in the positioning process.

I'd like to thank some of the people who've believed in me during my professional journey—who encouraged and supported my work. You have all helped make my career the enjoyable and successful ride that it continues to be.

First and foremost, I want to thank my cousin, marketing colleague, and longtime creative writing partner, Ed Shankman. It has been a pleasure seeing him employ his unwavering instinct for, and his deep understanding of, the principles of marketing over the years.

Of course I need to thank my wife, Judy Tomlinson, and my family: my parents, Sarah and Leon, my children, Kim and Matt, my grandchildren, Max and Wes, and my sister, Emily.

Then, in no real order, I'd like to show my great appreciation for my mentor, Larry Stern; for Linda Sadler and Guy Dess, who hired and then rehired me at the agency that was then called CommonHealth, Inc. (now known as Ogilvy Health); for my good friend and occasional business "partner," Tim Brown; for my friend and occasional collaborator, Joe Gugliuzza; for my extraordinary and brilliant boss at Pace, Inc, Gary Gold; for my former client who then became my boss, Chuck Schneider; and for my current leading client, Lawrence Schau, who continues to give me opportunities to do my best work.

PART I

Getting Started

CHAPTER 1

The Remarkable Concept

This chapter will consider why brand positioning is foundational to effective marketing, and discuss how positioning is changing for a new era.

There's only one place to start.

Al Ries and Jack Trout are the geniuses who innovated the concept of market positioning more than 60 years ago. Here's the famous summation that some say birthed the entire field:

*Positioning is **not** what you do to a product. Positioning is what you do to the mind of the prospect. That is, you position (place) the product in the mind of the potential buyer. [1]*

This book builds on that remarkable idea. It also incorporates a wealth of related concepts developed by countless marketing experts in the decades since.

Yet surprisingly, after all that expert attention and effort, even today positioning isn't fully accepted in the business world. While many people recognize the power of the trailblazing ideas that Ries and Trout developed, I'm not sure their numbers would constitute a majority.

One reason may be that, according to Bhat and Reddy, positioning is an exceptionally complex concept, and one of the most challenging in all of marketing. [2]

Positioning is one of the most challenging concepts in all of marketing.

For my part, I've been quite lucky because, throughout my career, I've had clients and co-workers who appreciated the value that a clear, strong, and differentiating marketing position can deliver. Most have understood that if a brand or a business doesn't have that differentiator, the chances of achieving success will be dramatically reduced.

When I have the chance to work with those kinds of smart, capable people, I've repeatedly been able to employ the positioning process to great advantage.

However, I've also known many decision makers who simply do not and will not accept the benefits of the positioning process—any positioning process. Some of those folks seem to mostly view positioning as a semiacademic exercise—a thing experts say organizations *should* do, but whose value can be hard to prove to shareholders and boards of trustees.

Then there's another group of marketers and decision makers—ones who are at least open to the value of positioning, but can't be convinced to invest the energy, money, and time that's required to see it through in a rigorous and strategic way.

I can certainly sympathize with that latter group. Because, when done right, positioning is damn hard work. There's a lot to think about, and a lot of planning. There's a lot of research, and a lot of steps. Also, it can be very expensive—although it doesn't have to be.

In my experience, positioning is worth every bit of that effort. It's certainly not a waste of time or money. On the contrary, done right, it's actually one of the most valuable—and most measurable—activities a business can undertake.

Starting a Chain Reaction

This book is the culmination of a professional lifetime spent in boardrooms and business war rooms, marketing products of all kinds, for a wide range of organizations—some tiny, some absolutely huge.

The underlying premise of the book is that the principles and process of brand positioning are *essential* for brand and business success and, when positioning is done with discipline, it can bring your marketing to a whole other level.

But, you might ask, what are those principles? What is the process?

For the answer, let me quickly describe the way I think about a marketing position—any marketing position, for any product, service, or company. In my experience, it comes down to three interlinked elements which, I contend, are the building blocks of effective positioning:

- Identifying meaningful positive value;
- Differentiating;
- Making an emotional connection.

> Effective positioning is based on three building blocks.

Each of these elements is essential. And, if you know the positioning field, you'll recognize that the last one is quite new. The need for that new element and its vital importance will be discussed throughout the pages that follow.

***

Use these building blocks to create an effective marketing position and you will set off a chain reaction that propagates into and through the brand development process, and which will impact everything you do with the brand: the color scheme, the logo, the imagery, the messaging, the promotion, and all the tactics that follow.

Employ these building blocks to create your position, and you will gain extraordinary marketing power—whatever field you're in, whatever product, brand concept, or business you're attempting to promote.

Becoming a Leader

Ries and Trout's book, *Positioning: The Battle for Your Mind,* was first published in 1981, more than a decade after they first began collaborating on articles about the subject. When Ries and Trout finally got around to collecting all their insights in one book, it was revolutionary.

In fact, Philip Kotler wrote exactly that, asserting that positioning "is the revolutionary concept that Al Ries and Jack Trout introduced in their now classic book." [3]

Ries and Trout said it was possible to become a leader in your field simply by following their approach. What a radical idea!

Their thesis assumes that you, as a marketer, already understand and follow other basic marketing principles. For example, they don't talk much about the "four Ps"—product, place, price, and promotion—probably surmising that you already take those basic marketing components into account.

The book you have in your hand also doesn't focus on the four Ps. Now, no one would suggest that they can be ignored—not if you want your marketing effort to have a chance of success. In fact, anyone who is in business ignores those Ps at their peril.

But even Philip Kotler, considered by many to be the father of modern marketing, has recognized that there is something fundamental lurking behind the Ps, something that, in effect, relegates them to a subordinate role.

Here's what Kotler said in his introduction to a revised edition of Ries and Trout's original book: [4]

> For years, all of us in marketing taught our students to build a marketing plan around the "four Ps"—Product, Price, Place, and Promotion. I began to realize some years ago that important steps needed to precede the four Ps.
>
> Positioning is a revolutionary idea precisely because it cuts across the other four Ps. It **informs** each of the Ps and adds consistency to them.
>
> [bold emphasis added]

Kotler goes on to explain why those important steps are so foundational. In summary, he says:

> Positioning can affect the product.
> Positioning can affect the price of the product.
> Positioning can affect the place the product is sold.
> Positioning can affect the promotion of the product.

When Kotler says that positioning "informs" each of the Ps, I believe he is using understated language, probably because he is advancing what, for him, must have been a radical admission. What he is implying, but not asserting, is one of the main themes of this book—that the *product, service, or organization's marketing position is the bedrock on which every aspect of the marketing of that product, service, or organization must be built.*

Let me rephrase that:

To maximize success, every single aspect of a product, service, or organization's marketing must be fully and completely aligned with its marketing position.

I'll be exploring that idea—that central, guiding idea—throughout the following pages.

It's also important to note that Kotler asserts, "… positioning is not only alive and well today, but also a powerful tool for creating and maintaining real differentiation in the marketplace." [5]

Positioning cuts across the four Ps.

He's certainly right that positioning is alive and well. The amount of material currently available—including many follow-on books by Ries and/or Trout—that addresses positioning in one way or another is too voluminous to measure.

And yet, there is still a significant gap. The reality is that almost all of that extensive material, while mostly helpful and often very insightful, is predominantly quite abstract. You can read it, digest it, understand it, and still not know how to get the tangible, practical results you need. Few experts have bothered to develop a step-by-step system, a workable process that shows how to create a viable, strategically-effective marketing position. You can search far and wide and not find a detailed, unified methodology that enables you, the marketer, to implement positioning in pragmatic, real-world-actionable terms. Certainly not one that has been generally accepted.

Are you seeking to accomplish effective positioning in your *specific* situation using all three of the building blocks noted earlier?

Do you aspire to a leadership position in your category (or in your career)?

If you follow this book's process, *it doesn't matter* what kind of business you're in. It makes no difference where your product is in its life cycle. Whoever you are, whatever your product, regardless of what you do in the business world, if you use this system with real rigor and consistency—with discipline—your success will increase.

In these pages, you will see how the building blocks work together to form a clear, logical, and exceptionally effective positioning process. This guidebook will show you how the positioning process can and will define the best path forward for your product or brand or business.

I call the process positioning with power.

And wow, is it powerful.

Key Takeaways

- Positioning is one of the most challenging concepts in all of marketing.
- Effective positioning is based on three building blocks.
- Positioning cuts across the four Ps of marketing and serves as the foundation for each of them.

PART II

The Foundations of Positioning

CHAPTER 2

Defining Positioning

To work successfully with brand positioning, we have to first establish a definition of the concept that is adapted to today's marketing environment.

Let's make sure we understand **what positioning is**.

Today, decades after Ries and Trout published their pioneering book, you might reasonably expect a consensus definition of positioning would exist by now. Yet, despite the fact that it is widely acknowledged as one of the most important concepts in the entire business field, positioning remains extraordinarily hard to define, even for many experienced and highly successful marketers.

This duality was highlighted by Kalafatis, Tsogas, and Blankson who said that "a single, universally accepted definition [of positioning] has yet to emerge." [6]

Quite recently, Natasha Saqib of India's University of Kashmir underscored this reality, writing that, while it

> ...is generally accepted that theoretically, practically, and strategically positioning has become one of the key components in modern marketing management, ...there has been no single universally accepted definition of the concept of positioning...[even] the boundaries of the concept are often not clearly defined. [7]

That situation hasn't kept definitions and versions and approaches from proliferating endlessly.

In an effort to find a unifying definition, many business writers have offered unhelpful versions that go something like this:

> Positioning is how a business achieves a clear, unique, and advantageous position.

Whenever you try using a term to define itself, you know you've got problems.

Despite the murkiness around the concept, business and marketing experts all over the globe vigorously affirm the foundational nature of positioning. Kalafatis et al., for example, have asserted that "the concept of positioning has become one of the fundamental components of modern marketing management" and, importantly, that "evidence…indicates a positive relationship between company performance (in terms of profitability and/or efficiency) and well-formulated and clearly defined positioning activities." [8]

Positioning undergirds an effective marketing mix.

Saqib agrees and goes even further, emphasizing that "positioning decisions determine the direction of a firm's overall marketing strategy and…an effective marketing mix can only be developed once a company has crafted a distinct positioning strategy." [9]

To put an even finer point on it, G. P. Dovel contended that positioning shouldn't just be one aspect of a marketing strategy, but rather it should serve as the backbone of any business plan. [10]

Extensive scholarly explorations address the value of positioning in great depth, and many knowledgeable authors have offered their own carefully conceived definitions. Yet the consensus view seems to be that, despite all the effort, no one has really improved on Ries and Trout's original formulation.

So let's take another look at the way they put it. Again, here's what Ries and Trout say:

*Positioning is **not** what you do to a product. Positioning is what you do to the mind of the prospect. That is, you position (place) the product in the mind of the potential buyer.*

This version is clear, it's concise, and it's authoritative. It undoubtedly could serve as the basis for a productive, effective positioning process, although such a process has remained elusive down through the years.

As well-accepted and authoritative as their definition is, I have little choice but to take issue with it.

I don't take this step lightly. However, after my many, many years working actively in the field, as well as extensive research and a careful study of the diverging perspectives on the topic, I've come to believe in an updated approach.

My approach shares a great deal with the original, but is drastically different in at least one essential way. To understand the basis for it, we first need to fully grasp what Ries and Trout were advancing.

In their book, they were quite assertive about the principles they were advocating. They said:

> To be successful today, you must touch base with reality. And the only reality that counts is what's already in the prospect's mind. The basic approach of positioning is not to create something new and different, but to manipulate what's already up there in the mind...
>
> Our (society's) extravagant use of communication...has so jammed our channels that only a tiny fraction of all messages actually gets through.... *The only answer to the problems of an over-communicated society is...positioning.... (To) cut through the traffic jam in the prospect's mind...* [11]
>
> [Italic emphasis added]

Ries and Trout made it plain—repeatedly—that their entire focus was the mind. That only by appealing to the rational, thinking brain could a viable position be established. Even in later revisions to the book and updates to the concept, Ries and Trout (and also Trout on his own) asserted that the sole purpose of positioning is to connect products and services with the mind of the audience.

Brilliant and groundbreaking as their work was, in doing so, they missed something.

Something BIG.

By focusing on mental processes, they have *almost entirely bypassed the third building block* introduced in Chapter 1. Here again are those three interlinked elements, which I've found to be the building blocks of effective positioning:

- Identifying meaningful positive value;
- Differentiating;
- Making an emotional connection.

And, as I said earlier, *each of these elements* is essential. To ignore the third building block would be like leaving off the third leg of a three-legged stool.

***

These days, it has begun to dawn on marketers across the planet—whatever their business situation might be—that stimulating real emotion in their audience is a critical factor in successful marketing.

Marketers in every field seem to be increasingly recognizing that it's not only essential to appeal to the head; they are realizing that effective marketing also connects with the heart.

Now, I want to be absolutely, crystal clear about this, because this new marketing emphasis can be misused and abused, and so my point could be easily misunderstood. I'm *not* advocating for the manipulation of people's emotions. I'm of course well aware that such manipulation happens—in fact, it seems to be an increasingly prevalent part of the communications landscape, with everyone from product promoters and pastors to politicians preying on people's fears, hopes, and dreams. To ignore that reality would be naïve in the extreme.

But it's important to stress that I'm *not* talking about this type of manipulation in this book.

Instead, I've always believed in working with positive attributes—positive value. I always strive to make a positive approach to the audience. In my work, I've consistently employed that positive mindset. I believe, as a result, I've been able to successfully establish *genuine and sincere* emotional connections to all sorts of audiences in a wide range of fields, from health care and high tech to automobiles and accounting.

This extensive experience has shown me unequivocally that making that *genuine and sincere* emotional connection will not only "cut through the traffic jam in the prospect's mind," as Ries and Trout describe; this positive approach will not only gain the consumer's attention in the short term, it will also maintain it in the long term.

And that's what I mean when I advocate for connecting with the heart.

The fact is that emotional resonance can help to build a genuine, potentially permanent, relationship with the consumer, and it should be employed toward that end in every case.

What's more, it's true beyond the shadow of a doubt that the stronger the emotional connection, the more lasting the relationship will be.

***

The basis for these ideas is explored in more depth later on, and I'll touch on fascinating data about recent scientific advances that lend this approach great credence. But I want to state my basic intention plainly here at the outset. This book is intended to build on the original—and essential—ideas developed by Ries and Trout, *and take those ideas an important additional step beyond.* These pages will show how the "three building blocks" approach I've adopted and implemented during my career can lead all of us to a new understanding of—and ability to make more effective use of—market positioning.

To get us started down that road, I'll share the definition of positioning I use—a new definition that incorporates these vital insights.

> Taking positioning an important step beyond.

Like the Ries and Trout original, my definition is clear and concise, and most people I've worked with have found it easy to understand. As I've been suggesting, however, my definition differs from the originators' in an absolutely fundamental way. Specifically, it incorporates *all* of the above mentioned three building blocks. Here is my version:

*Positioning is how you **differentiate** the **value** of your products and services **in a positive way** that not only places the product in the mind of the prospect but also **deeply, emotionally connects** with your target.*

I'd like you to take a few minutes and think about that, and I'd especially like you to note and ponder the similarities and differences between the two definitions.

As we dig further into it, we'll see how helpful the similarities will be as we make practical use of the positioning concept in the real world.

And we'll also see how the differences give positioning a new kind of power.

***

Before going further, there's one important thing to note. As many readers will be aware, there is a significant distinction between *market positioning* and a *positioning statement* (which is sometimes known as a "positioning platform").

The definitions in the preceding section describe what a marketing position is, but they don't tell you about positioning statements.

A positioning statement is an articulation of the marketing position. It should (and typically does) follow a preestablished formula or structure. To illustrate the difference, let's start with an example of a marketing position that I'll invent for a well-known brand:

BMW is the make of automobile built to meet the needs of driving aficionados.

That phrase does "place the product in the mind of the potential buyer," as Ries and Trout recommend. It also presents the differentiated, positive value in a way that connects with the target audience. So it meets the building block requirements and abides by my definition.

Now, let's look at an example of a positioning statement that could derive from that marketing position. (Note: Again, this is entirely my own invention. It follows the format I use when building positioning statements for my clients. The application of this format is explored in detail in Chapter 6.)

Among automobile manufacturers, BMW is the make that gives car owners an exhilarating driving experience because it delivers unbeatable performance, technological perfection, luxurious appointments, and a unique approach to automotive design. Drivers feel a thrill every time they take the car on the road.

Okay, looking at that, you might say, "Wow, that positioning statement is a mouthful. How are we supposed to use that in advertising and promotion?"

The answer is, you're not. *Definitely not.* In fact, it's important to recognize that your positioning statement is intended *only* to support your internal team's understanding of where your product, service, or brand concept fits in the marketplace. It provides the foundation for messaging, but it is NOT messaging.

I'll repeat this because it can be a source of confusion: Your positioning statement is NOT outward-facing messaging—yet, it absolutely MUST serve as the underlying basis for message development and promotion. In fact, it will not only lead to your messaging, it will give you the basis for every single promotional step you take. You'll see how and why as you read on.

The positioning statement has to be lengthy because it includes key reasons to believe—which, as we will see, form a vital part of the statement.

To look at how this works in practice, let's look one more time at the positioning statement I derived from BMW's marketing position:

Among automobile manufacturers, BMW is the make that gives car owners an exhilarating driving experience because it delivers unbeatable performance, technological perfection, luxurious appointments, and a unique approach to automotive design. Drivers feel a thrill every time they take the car on the road.

Keeping that in mind, then consider how effortlessly the company's promotional message flows from this positioning statement.

I'll bet you already know it—because it's one of the most well-known promotional messages in the history of advertising.

By following the positioning process presented in these pages, you'll see how you and your own marketing efforts can achieve that kind of powerful outcome.

Key Takeaways

- Positioning remains very hard to define.
- Positioning undergirds an effective marketing mix.
- It's time to take positioning an important step beyond.

CHAPTER 3

The Building Blocks of Positioning

Fully understanding the essential elements of brand positioning is necessary to implement an effective positioning process.

We're about to walk through the positioning process step-by-step and in detail (complete with real-world examples). To ensure maximum understanding, let's go back to review and expand on the building blocks I've been discussing.

They are as follows.

Building Block #1—Positive Value

Positive value is, of course, essential for any product or service. If your offering isn't contributing positive value to people's lives, you might consider quietly expunging it from the marketplace. Without positive value, it doesn't have much reason for being.

It's important to be clear that "value" in this context *definitely DOES NOT mean cost.* Instead, it's the tangible benefit, the product or service's attributes and usefulness, its overall desirability. To determine your product's value, you need to ask:

- What are my product's (or service's) genuine advantages?
- How effectively have I minimized any disadvantages?

One way to answer these questions is to analyze the four Ps mentioned earlier. That's how Kotler and many other marketing experts determine a product's value. They look at the product's attributes; gauge its pricing; evaluate its "place" or location; and then appraise its promotion and communication.

While this type of analysis is well-accepted and can be very beneficial, I've had great success using a different tool.

You may have heard of the SWOT (**S**trengths/**W**eaknesses/**O**pportunities/**T**hreats) analysis method.

SWOT is generally recognized as being highly effective and easy to use, a process that can help organizations large and small develop a much deeper and fuller awareness of the overall marketing situation. It works well whether you are promoting a product or service, a brand or a family of brands. It can even be used to analyze how an individual—or an individual's "brand"—can best interact with the marketplace.

Using SWOT is a lot like peeling a situational onion. It encourages us to dig down into the various ways the product or service delivers value, while at the same time bringing current and potential risks to the surface. In that way it bolsters both strategic planning and reality-based decision making.

When we do a SWOT analysis with *brutal* honesty and extreme granularity—and that's really the only way to do it if you're after the best results—the picture that emerges will almost always give you a fair and objective assessment of your product's value in the marketplace.

By the way, it will also distinctly clarify the four Ps for you at the same time.

***

It's essential to now address another key aspect of building block #1. Let's refer back to those previous two questions:

- What are my offering's genuine advantages?
- How effectively have I minimized any disadvantages?

These are both essential questions to be sure—but, in order to get the right answers, we need to answer one more, very different question.

That additional question is: "Who should be answering those first two questions?"

Who is best suited to determine your real-world advantages?

In other words, you and your organization need to figure out who can most accurately assess your offering's real-world advantages and disadvantages.

It seems like a no-brainer to me. If you hope to be genuinely responsive to the needs of your market, the answer must be, has to be, that your target audience—or, even more narrowly, the end consumer—is the one to make those determinations.

You have to ask your customers.

I recommend that business decision makers who intend to successfully market their offering to consumers make sure that those customers need, or at least want, what they are selling in the way they are selling it. And the obvious way to accomplish that is to ask them.

Sometimes this seems so basic to me as to be indisputable. Yet I can't tell you how many smart, experienced marketers and businesspeople are willing to simply skip this step. Some rationalize their decision by pointing to the time, energy, and money it takes to conduct quality research. Some look at what their competitors or potential competitors are doing and assume that all they have to do is make some improvements or do things differently, and the market will respond. Still others believe that they intuitively, instinctively grasp the will of the market.

I've worked with more than a few who fall into each of those groupings. And, to be honest, some of them have actually turned out to be right when they moved forward without advance confirmation from their audience.

But when people don't simply make assumptions, but rather do the research, when they ask the questions, they frequently not only gain a better sense of what the market prefers, but they often also learn something else, something important—how to better relate to their audience.

And many of my clients have discovered unexpected insights and other valuable data that they could never have guessed if they hadn't asked the questions.

Building Block #2—Differentiation

There are many ways to describe this aspect. But whether you call it…:

- Standing apart;
- The point of distinction;
- Separation from the pack;
- Finding a niche;
- And so on.

…differentiating your product or service is the central step in positioning—and some say it is the single most important action you can take on the road to success.

Typically, manufacturers and promoters emphasize attributes, features, and benefits to accomplish that differentiation, spending huge amounts of energy, time, and money to set their offerings apart from the competition.

However, attributes, features, and benefits are not the only way to create separation or distinction. Theodore Levitt, writing in the *Harvard Business Review*, argues that commodities can be set apart just as well as any other goods or services.

To explain this, he focuses on the idea of an offering, as opposed to a product or service.

Here is a summary of his approach:

There is no such thing as a commodity. All goods and services are differentiable. Though the usual presumption is that this is more true of consumer goods than of industrial goods and services, the opposite is the actual case.…

…for example, dealers in metals, grains, and pork bellies trade in…generic products. But what they "sell" is the claimed distinction of their execution—the efficiency of their transactions…their responsiveness to inquiries.… In short, the *offered* product is differentiated, though the *generic* product is identical. [12]

This insight may be counterintuitive at first. "Hold on," I can almost hear you say. "What does he mean, 'No such thing as a commodity?' Of course, there are commodities. What about sugar and salt?"

And, at the very same time you are formulating that question, I can also imagine you wondering something like, "How can a generic product be set apart from competitors? It's *generic!* By definition, that means it's identical!"

Again, the answer to both questions is in Levitt's last paragraph prior—and it's brilliant. As he says, it's not about the product, it's about the *offering*.

And he's right. The way any product or service, in fact, *every* product or service, is presented to the marketplace, and the way it impacts the marketplace, must be—*has to be, by definition*—different in *every single instance*. Even if two companies are selling the exact same product, it would be virtually impossible for them to sell it in exactly the same way, even if they wanted to.

> The *offering* is key to differentiation.

For example, one company might be based in Delaware, the other in Montana. There's a difference, right off the bat. Being based in those disparate locations will affect a range of factors: the supply chain, the way the product is sold, and the way it is purchased. Consider accessibility, for starters. If the product is made in Delaware, it's more accessible to more customers than one made in Montana simply because more people live nearby and more companies are based in shouting distance. Shipping costs will be lower, there may be more staff available to hire, and the level of employee talent may be better (of course, it could also be worse—but either way, it will unavoidably be different).

Or consider one product that's made by a conglomerate, and a competitor product made by a small, privately held company. Different kinds of differences in this scenario. But—and again, this can have major ramifications—the smaller company may have a smaller sales force of, let's say, hard-charging young college grads. The larger one has a larger staff, and let's say they're experienced, middle-aged women and men. Here, *in both cases*, a competitive advantage is *potentially* available—it all depends on how the company operates.

In both these examples, we are positing that the products are *exactly* the same, and that neither company is in any way better than the other in terms of producing the product itself—which is, of course, highly unlikely. But, even if that were true, the way the companies interact with their audiences—the way they attempt to deeply connect with them—can't help but be somewhat different. Probably significantly different, in fact.

As Levitt says, the difference can be "the claimed distinction of their execution." But, whatever the differences may be, the company that exploits those differences, demonstrates positive value, and then deeply connects with its audience, is the one that will inevitably be more successful.

Building Block #3—Emotional Connection

Positioning with power is simply more effective than any other positioning-related approach.

How can I say that? Because, in addition to being the underlying basis for your entire strategy (see Chapter 9), positioning with power also gives you the unerring ability to impactfully express your brand's emotion-based personality characteristics.

That expression of emotion is key. It's what breathes vitality into your product within the marketplace.

As we will soon see (and despite Ries and Trout's emphasis on the rational mind), the most important of the three positioning building blocks may be to identify and make use of the primary emotion aroused by your brand.

Expressing your brand's emotion-based personality is actually what transforms your offering from just any old product into a living, breathing, and durable brand—and, in some cases, a timeless one.

***

I'm going to be as definitive as I can be about this last point:

Making an emotional connection is the nexus of the positioning and branding process.

All positioning work leads up to that emotional connection, and every aspect of branding and promotion flows from it.

Emotion breathes vitality into your product.

If that is in fact true, it follows logically that *everything* that becomes an outgrowth of your marketing position—all of the branding, brand personality, messaging, and promotion—every aspect must also be emotion-based, or even emotion-focused.

***

Having placed all this emphasis on emotion, do I have any evidence for its value?

Let's start with the fact that marketers are increasingly recognizing the centrality of making emotional connections. For example, Valentin Saitarli, writing in *Forbes*, explained in detail why emotion is "The super weapon of marketing and advertising."

He wrote:

An analysis from the Institute of Practitioners in Advertising found that "purely emotional content performed about twice as well" as purely rational content. The…"touch to the heart," is what often makes a company and its product memorable.… [13]

Psychology Today, in an article written by Peter Noel Murray, PhD, posits the following (as Saitarli points out):

Functional magnetic resonance imaging (fMRI) shows that when evaluating brands, consumers primarily use emotions (personal feelings and experiences), rather than information (brand attributes, features, and facts).

Studies show that positive emotions toward a brand have a far greater influence on consumer loyalty than trust and other judgments, which are based on a brand's attributes.

Emotions are the primary reason why consumers prefer brand-name products.… A nationally advertised brand has power in the marketplace, because it creates an emotional connection to the consumer. [14]

So as marketers, why not aim to trigger the right feelings and make an emotional impression to attract attention to your product or service and boost sales?

Saitarli offers a compelling reason why so many people in our field are reluctant to move in this direction:

> …When our team brings emotional marketing to the table, we've found that *80 percent of our clients seem to doubt the strategy—until we deliver results.* [And this is true despite the fact that] campaigns with purely emotional content performed about twice as well as those with only rational content. [15]
>
> [Italic emphasis added.]

This testimony is particularly revealing. Even though Saitarli has the data and the know-how to build a strong case for the value of emotion, the decision makers he deals with continue to gravitate toward the cerebral.

My own experience also shows that the large majority of marketing clients need convincing of the viability emotional connection as a marketing tool.

So, to bolster the case Saitarli and I are making, let's take a quick side trip into the newly emerging field of consumer neuroscience.

F. Javier Otamendi and Dolores Lucia Sutil Martín of the Brain Research Lab at Spain's Universidad Rey Juan Carlos provide an excellent overview of this burgeoning field.

Here are excerpts from their recent article on the topic:

> …[P]roviding an emotional message…increases the audience's attention to the advertisement, and…enhances the product's appeal and generates a higher level of brand recall. Indeed, advertisements with emotional content are more likely to be remembered than those conveying news.
>
> The tools [that are documenting this include] virtual reality …functional magnetic resonance imaging, positron emission tomography…electroencephalography, magnetoencephalography,

transcranial magnetic stimulation, steady-state topography, …eye tracking, galvanic skin response, electromyography… [and] facial expression recognition. [16]

Consumer neuroscience is a young, fascinating, and expanding field of research. It has already begun demonstrating the potency of emotion in achieving advertising impact. And, since advertising is the most observable output of the positioning and branding processes, it's only logical to believe that emotion is also central to those processes.

Considering the Competition

If you're successful at constituting those building blocks—identifying the way your product offers positive value; focusing in on what makes it separate and distinct from any other product in your market or category; and then effectively utilizing those aspects to make an emotional connection with your audience—if you do those things well, it's reasonable to expect that you will achieve a competitive advantage.

But, when you do so, you are actually likely to experience something else, and it's something extraordinarily important. When the building blocks are in place and, as I'm suggesting, you have established a strong, reality-based marketing position with your customers, you may find that *you really don't have to worry about the competition.*

Of course you need to keep an eye on them, and I'll explain what that means in a little bit. But you won't need to keep both eyes on them. They don't need to be the focus of your thinking.

Why? Because effective positioning has so much power.

I'll even go so far as to say:

If you manage your positioning properly, competitors need not be feared.

The key to that formulation clearly is, *"If you manage your positioning properly."*

If you do, it can be like donning impermeable armor as you suffer the slings and arrows of the marketplace.

"But," you might say, "of course every business needs to fear its competitors." My answer is, actually, no, you don't have to fear them—in fact, don't fear them; investigate them instead. Then analyze what you learn about them carefully and thoroughly. Examine them in the same detailed way you will be analyzing so much information throughout the positioning process.

If you do, if you pay attention to what the competition is doing—and do your best to anticipate their initiatives whenever possible—you will find that, just as every human alive makes mistakes, every business on the planet has a weakness. Or maybe several.

Your competitors do too.

In fact, as we will see, while boosting your strengths and minimizing your own weaknesses are central to clarifying your marketing position, uncovering your competition's foibles can also bring significant rewards.

One key benefit of the positioning process is that it typically uncovers a multitude of opportunities for achievement, and those opportunities frequently open doors to growth. You will learn a tremendous amount about your own business (as well as your competitors) when you go through the positioning steps; and that deep understanding of your strengths and your competitors' weaknesses almost always highlights obvious, if often unexpected, growth opportunities.

Having a healthy attitude toward the competition is so important, so central to effective marketing, that we're going to stop right here and let you think about that accentuated statement.

Here it is again:

If you manage your positioning properly, competitors need not be feared.

A detailed discussion of this vital topic comes later in this book.

However, now's the time to move forward with the positioning and branding process—step by thoughtful step.

Key Takeaways

- Your customers are best suited to determine your real-world advantages.
- The offering is key to differentiation.
- Emotion breathes vitality into your product.
- Analyze your competitors, don't fear them.

PART III

How to Position Your Brand, With Power

CHAPTER 4

Positioning Step I

Analysis

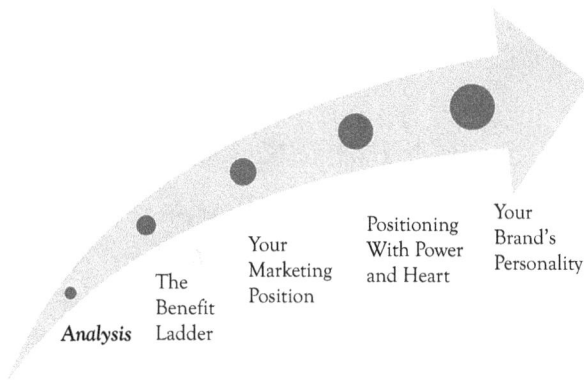

Figure 4.1 Five-step positioning process, highlighting step one

Conducting an extensive situational analysis is the first step in the brand positioning process.

Okay. We're ready to start the positioning work in earnest.

Here are the essential actions to take in step one of the positioning process (Figure 4.1).

1. Key audience(s) analysis and segmentation;
2. Situational analysis;
3. Communications review;
4. Competitive and macroenvironmental analysis;
5. External research and interviews with potential customers.

As indicated before, analysis deserves a great deal of attention, and that's why the chapter you're in is one of the longer chapters in this book. In my experience, the more thorough the upfront analysis, the more effective the following steps will be. Conversely, no matter how capable and qualified your marketing team, if they don't have access to essential, in-depth information, they are almost guaranteed to struggle on the back end.

While analyses can take time and cost money—as does every single one of the foundational steps included in this book—analytical efforts pay such handsome dividends that I always recommend making the investment. Not every organization does so, but those that do consistently realize major dividends.

Analysis Part 1: Key Audiences

As noted before, if you hope to be genuinely responsive to the needs of your audience members, *you need to talk with them.* Note I didn't say, "talk **to** them." You should be interacting with them, listening to their input, understanding their desires and preferences as thoroughly as you practically can.

Your target audience (or the end consumer) should be one of your key resources; they can be an ongoing source of data and insight to help you clarify or even determine the positive value your product offers in the marketplace.

In other words, to connect with your market, you need to know who the market is and what they need from you. This may seem obvious, but it's shocking how many major corporations launch brands and go to market with a limited understanding of who they're trying to reach and what they're all about.

Your audience should be a key resource.

Depth of analysis is what you're after, whenever possible. Dig as deep as you can and you will have a real chance of comprehending your audience. Accomplish that, and you will have taken a major step toward creating an effective, successful marketing effort.

Segmentation and Personas

It's vital to recognize the direct relationship between audience analysis and the process of market segmentation. Once you have achieved a workable understanding of your audience as described previously, you can begin to segment them into groups or personas or customer profiles. Such groupings can make use of demographic, psychographic, and behavioral data. In some cases, they can even use such esoteric data as firmographics and technographics.

These techniques help you shape your marketing position, and can also pinpoint how to communicate with your target audience more effectively when you get to that stage.

Segmentation is becoming increasingly available to even small companies and organizations through the increasing accessibility of advanced marketing technology. That technology is, of course, a broad and complex topic all on its own.

While these are large topics and aren't within the scope of this book, if we are going to truly understand our audiences, we do need to consider three types of analyses that are related to segmentation development processes.

A. Demographics

To start—and regardless of whether you are trying to reach consumers, business people, or opinion leaders, whoever your target may be—you need to know as much demographic information as possible. Most marketers include age, gender, income, ethnicity, and marital status in their demographic analyses. And, in case you're wondering if those factors apply to a business audience, the answer is yes—although, again, that may come under the heading of firmographics and, possibly, technographics.

You also need to know if the audience is local, regional, or national (or international). And details about their specific geographic location can also be essential, depending on the type of product and other aspects of the marketing situation.

B. Psychographics

According to Merriam-Webster, psychographics are ways of classifying population groups according to psychological variables such as attitudes, values, or fears. Other sources describe psychographics as analytics that explore the attitudes, interests, personality, values, opinions, and lifestyle of your target market.

Psychographic analysis often uses advanced data management tools. When applied thoughtfully, it can produce some of the most valuable information any marketer can have.

Why? Psychographic studies go beyond the age, gender, occupation/income, culture, and family status analysis of standard demographics and try to identify the under-the-surface beliefs and emotions of an audience. Done right, these studies can also tell you the reasons why audience members make specific decisions. And there is little more important than understanding the psychology and decision-making characteristics of your customers if you are going to make deep, powerful connections.

Just imagine if you could crawl inside a consumer's head and experience and understand their thoughts and feelings as they decide to use your product, or not use it. What a treasure trove of information that would give you! And that is what psychographics, when effectively done, is designed to supply.

C. Audience Behavior

Analyzing overt audience behavior is another way of deepening our understanding of audiences and how they are segmented in various ways. This type of analysis can be conducted in parallel to and be supportive of psychographic analysis. It tells you what your audience is doing, instead of why they are doing it.

Take, for example, an audience segment that behaves in this way:

- Shops at organic grocery stores;
- Spends a lot of money on travel;
- Volunteers at a climate-change organization;
- Logs into several news apps on a daily basis.

Looking at this list, you're already starting to have a picture of that kind of person, aren't you? And, if you're already able to form that picture, consider that you're doing so with a very small number of data points.

So, even though you don't know exactly how old they are, where they live, or other demographic information, and you have no psychographic information at all, working with only four behavioral aspects, you still have enough information to craft the start of a picture about the audience.

Today's technology is multiplying the power of behavioral analysis, and the technology is becoming more powerful all the time. I've worked with high-tech teams that obtained detailed data about an audience segment's behavior and were then able to extrapolate from those behaviors to build the profile of a specific type or types of persons (i.e., the "personas") within the given audience—even provide a picture of their emotional state in some cases. Based on this, we were then able to tailor our marketing position and anticipate how those people would react to our strategies, our branding activities, and our messages.

***

As should be obvious, a combination of basic demographics, psychographics, and behavioral data can be very powerful. However, even when your data (or your technological resources) are limited, audience analyses—and the strategies that stem from them—can still be essential tools in your marketing toolbox.

To expand on this point, let's look at a quick case study about a financial services business I worked with years ago. I'll call them FSC.

FSC supplied sophisticated risk management software and related digital products to banks and other financial institutions. Their prior agency had been tasked with building credibility for an eventual initial public offering (or possible acquisition). On that basis, the agency's efforts focused in on the financial analyst community along with domestic and international business publications.

However, neither the offering nor the acquisition had occurred—at least in part because FSC wasn't showing sufficient strength on the bottom line. The company's leadership faced facts and decided that growing the business was now an urgent need. So I got to work.

This all happened in the era before digital tools were being employed in business-to-business (B2B) marketing. These were the days before the Internet, websites, and social media. FSC's suite of brochures was their chief client-facing communication, so we created a series of thematically related hard copy booklets. Each one focused on one of FSC's major products.

I began by identifying the audience, in as much detail as I could. With growth as the focus, the target audience was now completely different than what the public relations (PR) agency had been aiming at. It was clear that FSC wanted to quickly spur growth, so my job was to connect with and motivate the banks and financial companies, not the outside analysts or the financial media.

But which specific individuals did we need to reach within those targets? If we were going to successfully motivate major organizations to buy the products, it was essential to identify, very specifically, who we were talking to and on what basis the purchasing decisions were being made.

As often happens, the client did not allot the time or the budget to execute a truly in-depth audience analysis. However, company leadership did provide access to internal experts who had a good grasp of the audiences' characteristics and a sense of their psychology. These experts also described the aspects of the products that were important to the key audiences and why they mattered.

It turned out that the company needed to reach two very specific, but *very* different groups: C-suite decision makers and the banks' internal software techies.

What do tech staffers care about? A software product's overall capabilities, specific features and benefits, ease of use, shelf life, and so on.

What do decision-making executives care about? Mostly, about a software product's ability to boost productivity and save them money.

Obviously, these are very different interests. And the members of each group are dramatically different as well, in terms of training, age, life experience, and general mindset.

After we gathered the available data—and after I did some covert positioning work behind the scenes—the team at FSC and I made a key strategic marketing decision that led to a unique messaging approach. We would focus on both audiences at the same time, in a way that would reinforce how much each depended on the other—and how important FSC was to both.

We incorporated two closely related yet distinct messages into each of the brochures. The outer few pages of each booklet featured a motivational sales message aimed at the executives, along with a minimal amount of technical info; the inner pages—each piece's core—provided in-depth, detailed, highly technical descriptions about the specific product, using the kind of language that made the tech staff comfortable.

Each brochure in the series took this approach and was highly effective at:

- Quickly conveying an exciting sales message to the executives;
- Showing the technical teams that we understood their concerns and were providing industry-leading solutions;
- Demonstrating that those technical advantages were so advanced and sophisticated that the company would virtually be committing malpractice if they weren't taken seriously.

The decision to package the tech-team-oriented content within a multipage "wrapper" that spoke to and motivated executive-level decision makers was unusual, to say the least. It turned out to be extraordinarily successful at reaching and connecting with both target audiences simultaneously.

> **NOTE** → In a book about positioning, it's important to reiterate that the covert positioning work done for this client was not part of my assignment, and this is sometimes the case. Yet, whenever budget, timing, and resources allow, I approach each situation by keeping positioning in the forefront of my mind. The reason is simple. Every marketing step an organization takes will, almost unavoidably, be based on its position.

Because of the distinctive approach we took—based on the positioning—FSC's brochures (and other related and fully aligned communications) conveyed a very strong and clear message: yes, FSC took their clients' decision makers very seriously, but they were equally concerned about their clients' technical staffs.

And, in the same way a more overt positioning process would have, I made sure that FSC's overall mindset and approach (as expressed in their brochures), included the three building blocks of positioning. The mindset we instituted accomplished the following:

- Demonstrated the value FSC offered, in both "executive speak" and very technical language;
- Clearly differentiated the company from the competition (given that their competitors had never implemented this kind of dual-track approach);
- Made a strong emotional connection with FSC's audiences by showing that the company understood and was responsive to clients' concerns at all levels.

To say the effort was successful would be an understatement. Building on the highly effective work of the PR agency—they had placed 50 major stories in *American Banker* and another 50 in other leading international banking trade publications, as well as achieving more than 500 citations in financial media—FSC revenues grew to more than $40 million.

Three years after I was brought in, one of the world's largest international software corporations offered almost $150 million to acquire the company. The former FSC today remains part of that conglomerate's financial services division.

Analysis Part 2: Marketing Situation

Marketing budgets are always tight. That's a fact of life that most agencies (and of course independent marketers and consultants) have to face on a pretty continuous basis. That fact means that clients are often resistant to implementing a comprehensive (and potentially, though not always, costly) strategic process.

This is especially true for those who don't fully grasp the value such a process delivers.

So I wouldn't be surprised if some people advise you to skip over or minimize some of the steps that are included in this book when you work with your clients or your employer. Or they might suggest that you just get done what you absolutely *must* do. "Just do the essentials," they might say. "Leave it at that."

I'm not going to agree with either of those thoughts.

Frankly, there's a right way and a wrong way to work toward your marketing goals, and we marketers should always try to do what's right for our clients. I say this not necessarily because we are altruists. The more compelling reason comes down to practical self-interest.

I'll put it simply:

Following marketing best practices will deliver the best bottom line results.

And when that happens, you can end up looking really good, along with everyone else involved.

So, when the powers that be, as in the case of FSC, hesitate to spend the amount of time and money needed to deliver great results, it's up to us to do our best to convince them. And explaining the value of the positioning process needs to be part of that conversation.

***

Let's focus on the next step: conducting a situational analysis.

This step is about as important as any single thing a marketer can do. So, again—if we can put budget and timing concerns to the side— let's just say that doing a complete and thorough situational analysis is vital.

Similar to what was noted earlier, some of the most valuable input a marketing agency or an independent marketer can obtain for this step can be sourced directly from the companies and brand teams they are working with. We marketers obviously can't know the client's industry, products, or audiences as thoroughly as its own staff does—although it's certainly part of our task to try. So, when staff members are available to supply inside information about their own markets, it's always in our best interest to listen.

And then we should confirm that information as far as possible on our own.

Why? Because the internal staff will undoubtedly have their own agendas. In many cases, they will want to make themselves look good at the expense of providing an unvarnished picture of the situation. In other cases, they may have been taught to parrot the company line, even when it doesn't match up with reality.

Whatever the reason or motivation, inaccurate market data is always an obstacle to our efforts. And, honestly, it's a major hurdle in the way of the client's potential success.

Accurate market data is essential.

In many instances, clients are reluctant to supply an in-depth download of some of this key information to an agency or independent marketer. I suggest pushing a little harder for it. I can't tell you how many times clients have thanked me after they shared this information.

With a little prodding.

It's always in an organization's self-interest to support a marketer when she or he is trying to do the job the right way.

***

Situational analysis is also sometimes called a *marketing audit*; however, the audits I've done have been a much more in-depth process. This is a handbook focused on positioning and branding—and also, aspects of the auditing process are treated to one degree or another elsewhere in this book—so I won't cover them in depth here.

But, in case you're curious, let's mention the key characteristics of a good audit:

- An understanding of the industry, and the company's standing within the industry;
- A sense of how the company sees itself vis-à-vis its customers and its competition; how that perspective may have changed in the past;
- If that perspective has in fact changed, gain an understanding of why it changed, and how that might impact the company's current status;
- A strong grasp of how the specific brand you are promoting fits in with the industry and the company;
- An understanding of the company's internal marketing structure and environment;

- Detail about the company's strengths and weaknesses, as well as its opportunities in the current (and future) environment, and any potential threats to its success. As previously mentioned, this is called a SWOT analysis;
- Market research (of various types) with both customers and prospects.

That's a quick overview, but a high-quality, in-depth audit can include so much more. Given today's marketing environment, for example, a thorough exploration of the burgeoning world of digital marketing and social media will also be required if we're going to say we've done our due diligence.

***

The type of situational analysis needed for the positioning process is typically somewhat limited compared to a full audit. Here's how it goes, when it's done well.

Start by scoping out the basic marketing situation through independent preresearch. This exploration should be as broad and deep as budget and time allow—and the Internet obviously these days can make this step faster and easier.

Then, based on this initial investigation, create a set of key questions; these should be the ones you believe absolutely *must* get answered. It often helps to review an initial list of these questions with company leadership to make sure the scope of the questions is complete but doesn't go into irrelevant topics or details.

Translate this material into a functional questionnaire, then conduct a download with as many members of the internal staff as is practical, and that the company is willing to make available. For these downloads, I always prefer individual interviews, either in-person or video chat. These offer the chance to read attitudes and body language and, at times, to ask additional questions on the fly. Talking to people individually also prevents the possibility of groupthink while providing an opportunity to compare and contrast various data points and perspectives.

***

Here are the kinds of questions we ask during these downloads, although they have to, of course, vary depending on the specific market and the details of the marketing situation:

- How does the organization or brand see its place in the market?
- What problem is the organization or brand designed to solve, or in what other way does it work to deliver positive value?
- How effectively does it accomplish that task?
- What is the organization or brand's own single-most pressing need or problem? What other needs or problems is it facing?
- How long has it been in this situation?
- What steps have already been taken to address the situation? Why did they work or not work, and to what degree?
- Who are the primary competitors and how are they impacting the organization or brand?
- Why has the organization engaged in this analysis and what are the expectations and measures of success?
- What is the budget?
- What is the time frame?

It can be interesting to see how the answers to these kinds of questions can differ from one interview to another, even within the same department, as various players present their perspectives. And the differences can be highly instructive of the internal dynamics within the organization, which can (and should), in turn, help to inform how you go about your work.

In some cases, a second round of these interviews is helpful to add depth and additional substance to the overall picture. Additional rounds are rarely needed.

***

When the internal interviews are completed, additional external sources of data and information should be explored as fully as possible. This can mean conducting external market research and market testing; revisiting the Internet, using the newly obtained information as background; talking with outside experts and various industry contacts; reading articles and books—you name it. The intent is to gain the amount of understanding you need to accomplish the marketing goals, and not more than is needed.

Of course, budget is almost inevitably an issue. And time restrictions, which can relate to the project's timeline or, for example, the availability of expert sources, are also a common limiting factor. We're all working in the real world, so those constraints can't be ignored.

In any case, the goal is always to learn as much as you can as quickly as you can, and then confirm the information as effectively as is practical. Keep the project goal in mind, but be flexible. Do that, and, if your budget and timing is sensible, you should be able to stay on track in most cases.

Analysis Part 3: Communications Review

The next essential step in the evaluation process is a comprehensive communications review. This is largely an internal exploration. It requires access to both a wide range of internal communication materials and staff at various levels, starting with the communications team itself and (often) going up to top leadership.

Here are some of the questions we ask during such a review:

- What is the organization or brand saying about itself?
- How long has it been communicating the way it does?
- How has it been saying things that way?
- Why has it taken the approach it's been using?
- Why does it feel the need to change now?
- What are its communications goals now?
- Specifically, what does it believe its audiences need to know now?
- How is digital and social media being utilized?
- How about traditional media?
- What are the budgets and timelines?

Again, an important part of this step is to review all of the company's available marketing materials. Reviewing the way the company or organization has actually been interacting with its target audiences can reveal *a lot*. Delving into the reasons why it did so can tell even more.

Take the case of a medium-sized hospital in the northeast, for example. We'll call it Jersey General Hospital, or JGH.

I had spent about a decade and a half working in, and then consulting for, hospitals all around the New York metropolitan area, when I was commissioned to conduct an in-depth communications review by the chief executive at JGH. We didn't talk about strategic work, I was asked to do an overview, pure and simple. After my first pass, I was asked to dig a little deeper.

During a month-long investigation, I engaged with key hospital staff—at several levels, in a range of departments. It soon became obvious to me that certain of the hospital's clinical capabilities, while not being actively promoted, were having a very positive impact on the affected patients. One program in particular was really changing lives, yet it was flying largely under the radar.

The service I'm referring to was a nontraditional, but very effective, community-based approach to treating people with diabetes. As you may know, diabetes is one of the nation's most prevalent disease states. My interviews and research indicated that, if we could improve the service a bit around the margins and expand its reach, the diabetes service had unusual potential.

In fact, it became clear that, if the hospital played its cards right, there was a genuine opportunity to leverage this innovative program into a significant competitive advantage. I became convinced that the diabetes service had the potential to act as a springboard to boost the entire hospital's profile. For one thing, we found data showing that the service was not only impacting patients in the immediate area but was also starting to draw patients from the entire northern part of the state. And that region contained large numbers of people who had diabetes.

I brought my findings to the hospital CEO. He was a young, aggressive executive and he quickly recognized the opportunity. He charged me with finding a way to make the most out of the situation.

I'd already learned that, historically, the hospital had been narrowly focused on its local community. After some additional fact-gathering, I advised the CEO to leverage the diabetes service, using it as the "tip of the spear" in a more regional promotional approach. We soon developed a program offering that focused on diabetes and also actively and intentionally broadened general awareness of the hospital's other strengths, while communicating out to a more regional service area.

That approach quickly created a positive cycle. The diabetes service began expanding, and a domino effect was created that positively and measurably impacted other key patient services. Taken together, those enhanced offerings extended the hospital's service area both east and west across the state, and increased the hospital's outpatient and inpatient utilization.

I was then asked to consult with the hospital and its staff on a range of marketing and communication projects. I continued in that role until a full-time marketing director was brought on board.

Years later, the efforts we had made and the growth that resulted were notable factors in the successful merger of the hospital with one of the most prestigious medical systems in the region.

That eventual merger was the result of hard work by dozens of people, and I would not claim credit for making it happen. But it is undeniable that the path first opened up when the hospital took the time to evaluate how it was communicating with its market. This led directly to uncovering ways it was delivering positive differentiating value, and it effectively connected with its audiences as a result.

Analysis Part 4: Competition

If you know the enemy and know yourself, you need not fear the result of a hundred battles.

—Sun Tzu

We have met the enemy and he is us.

—Walt Kelly

As promised, here are more thoughts on dealing with the competition. Actually, I have quite a few things to say.

For starters, it's important to be clear that the same way it's essential to analyze and understand your audiences, your marketing situation, and your communications approach, it is absolutely vital to know your competitors as thoroughly as you can.

However—and as important as a complete and accurate competitive picture is to your opportunity for success—it may actually be more important to know yourself, as Sun Tzu intimates (and Walt Kelly sort of does as well). This is especially true in terms of understanding how your organization or your brand can most effectively fit into the marketplace.

Among the many key insights Ries and Trout offered in *Positioning*, I believe this one to be particularly notable. It goes basically like this:

If you don't clearly and effectively define your position in the market, the market will define it for you.

In practice, this means that positioning is an activity you absolutely *must not* ignore or leave to chance. If you don't grab hold of your positioning and make it central to your strategy, you leave yourself wide open to sabotage by your competitors as well as to misunderstanding or misrepresentation by everyone else.

For example, given the power of social media these days, consider what could happen if a completely erroneous yet damaging description of your product or service was to become embedded in the social conversation. Unless you already have a clearly delineated, distinctive, and well-established position in your market, that unflattering description *could begin to dominate* the conversation. Undoing the damage from that kind of situation can take weeks, months, or even years—it has happened. In some cases, the business was unable to fully recover.

And that doesn't even take into account the costs that might be needed to rebuild the brand, financial and otherwise.

Know yourself and know your market.

That's why I always recommend making the effort to ensure you have an accurate, candid, and totally realistic view of your own organization and its place in the market; that you convert that perspective into a positive position statement that sets you distinctly apart; and then leverage that positive, differentiating value into a deep connection with your audience.

To get that ball rolling, a SWOT analysis is an easy-to-use and extraordinarily effective tool.

By now you've noticed that I've mentioned SWOT a few times. Why? There are really so many reasons—but, again, the main ones are that it's fast, it's comparably easy, and it gets the job done in an extremely useful way.

You should use it.

Here, as adapted from businessmakeover.eu, is an example of what a SWOT looks like, in this case featuring an instantly recognizable company. [17]

Table 4.1 Strengths, Weaknesses, Opportunities, Threats example

	SWOT	Coca-Cola
	Helpful	*Harmful*
Internal	**Strengths** • World's largest market share in beverage • Strong marketing, advertising, and distribution • Customer loyalty • Bargaining power over suppliers • Social responsibility	**Weaknesses** • Dominant focus on carbonated drinks • Some negative publicity • High debt level due to acquisitions • Brand failures
External	**Opportunities** • Bottled water consumption growth • Increasing beverage consumption in growing markets • Growth through acquisition	**Threats** • Increased demand for healthy food and beverages • Water scarcity • Strong competition • Possible saturation of carbonated drinks market • Strong dollar

Looking at this SWOT (Table 4.1), you'll see how even one of the largest, most successful companies in the world—despite its obvious 800-lb gorilla-type strengths and the potential opportunities listed here—can still have glaring weaknesses, and be subject to significant threats and risks.

Going through a SWOT exercise honestly, unflinchingly, and bravely will inevitably uncover new ways of understanding your business. It can also open many potential doors. Some will be unexpected, and in a very good way.

If you not only conduct the exercise earnestly but also have the courage to include people who have different perspectives about your company, from within and without, the benefits of the SWOT process can be enormous. In fact, the key to maximizing the value of a SWOT is to include and encourage as many different points of view as is practical.

Here is a group of top line questions that can help you create an effective SWOT and provide a start toward a fruitful, in-depth analysis:

Strengths

- Which aspects of your business are most successful?
- How do you measure success?
- What are your main assets?
- What strategic advantages do you have?
- What competitive advantages do you have?
- What else do you have that can help overcome current and potential obstacles?

Weaknesses

- What does your business need?
- What is keeping you from getting those things?
- What needs improvement?
- In what way can those things be improved?
- How would that improvement be measured?
- Are there gaps in your strategy? In your assets? In your teams?
- What tactics could you employ to improve?

Opportunities

- How could the market's evolution benefit your business? In what way?

- Where is potential growth likely to happen?
- What can be done to enhance that growth?
- Are there ways to improve your visibility?
- Are there ways to improve your reputation?

Threats

- How could the market's evolution threaten your business? In what way?
- How are your competitors actively impacting your market? Your sales?
- Are new competitors on the horizon?
- Could technology change your business?
- Is your visibility or reputation at risk?
- Are you getting what you need from suppliers?

I've accomplished very successful SWOT analyses with clients in the course of a couple of long afternoons, often with a day or two separating the sessions to let things marinate a bit.

I almost always find that SWOT is like peeling an onion. The types of questions mentioned earlier, while very useful in themselves, tend to lead to more questions, and then even more. The overall effect is a deep analysis that opens up significant insights, which frequently create great value.

And, of course, that kind of deep and valuable analysis can take time. So, depending on how far down the rabbit hole you're willing to go, consider setting aside a few more hours for this effort than you might think you'll need.

Or, if you're willing…maybe a lot more.

***

It's important to remember at all times that the goal of a SWOT, or any similar analysis, is to seek potential advantages for your business or brand—things that add differentiating positive value. You also want to look for any barriers you may face within your market.

After you have a clear and very honest picture of your own situation—and, I strongly advise, *ONLY AFTER* you have that—it's time to investigate the competition.

It's worth mentioning here one surprising perspective, primarily because it was voiced by someone who should know: Jeffrey Wilke, former CEO of Worldwide Consumer at Amazon. Here's what Wilke said in 2017: "I'm focused on customers and not competitors. Competitors' strategy changes all the time. We don't want to distract ourselves from customers by obsessing over what competitors are doing or not doing." [18]

Interesting viewpoint, right? However, while I completely agree that your own audience absolutely is your primary concern, and while I also believe that "obsessing" is going way too far, I *don't* agree that your competitors can be completely ignored. I guess it's possible that you could get away with it if you happen to be Amazon—but even that behemoth has competition, and I'd be shocked if they weren't doing a substantial amount of ongoing market intelligence, just in case.

Ideally, your competitive analysis will deliver a coherent and comprehensible view of your direct *and indirect* competitors' marketing strategies. It also tells you the ways they are executing specific tactics such as marketing, pricing, and distribution.

In some respects, a competitive analysis is a positioning exercise in reverse. Instead of identifying your own company's differentiating value, you now work to understand each competitor's value propositions and differentiators. Done well, it will provide many opportunities to learn your market in greater depth. It may also spark some new and creative ideas.

And that's never a bad thing.

The content of a competitive analysis can vary somewhat widely, based on your business goals. It can be as narrow as evaluating a competitor's web strategy, or as broad a 30,000-foot view of their overall marketing approach.

Given that this book is addressing big-picture topics like positioning and brand personality, I'm working with the broader definition.

"Great," you say, "I can see why we should do a thorough competitive review. Are you going to tell us how?"

Gladly.

Here are the key things you want to learn during an effective competitive analysis:

- What are the company/brand's primary characteristics?
- Who are their target customers?
- Are they the same or different than yours?

- If they're different, in what ways—and why has the competitor made that choice?
- If they're the same, are they approaching the customers in the same way you would?
- If yes, how effectively are they making use of that approach?
- If they're not, why not?
- Who are in the key management roles?
- What are those individuals' strengths and weaknesses?
- What key features and benefits do they highlight in their promotional efforts?
- What are their product price points?
- Have they received any funding or venture capital?
- How much? From whom? How was the capital secured?
- What is the state of their financial health?
- How are they capitalized?
- What are the strengths and weaknesses of their products and services?
- What is their marketing and sales strategy?

These are the primary items, although the list could go on for a while. I'm stopping here because, as I've mentioned about many aspects of these analytical steps, a competitive analysis can easily become a rabbit hole. The best approach is, when you feel that you have a good grasp of your competitors, particularly in terms of the threat(s) they represent and the opportunities they open up *for you*, stop there. You can always come back and gather more information. The fact is that many successful companies make competitive analysis an ongoing process.

"Okay, thanks," you say. "But where do I get the answers to all of those questions?"

Start with publicly available information sources, including websites, media articles, marketing materials, and so on. It may surprise you to realize how much useful data companies reveal, both intentionally and inadvertently, in public-facing documents.

Ask yourself why they included what they did. What did they leave out? If it were you, why would *you* include and exclude that kind of info? Do your best to extrapolate from these sources—tremendous value can be derived if you put in the time, effort, and energy.

The important thing actually is less about gathering reams of information; it's about getting enough insight that you can put yourself in your competitors' shoes. If you can understand the mindset behind the information they provide and gain insight into their thinking, you will already have a significant opportunity to gain a competitive advantage.

You can also contact competitors' customers and former employees, and many companies do this routinely. Other sources can include consultant briefings as well as Securities and Exchange Commission (SEC) filings, where applicable.

Analysis Part 5: External Research

While external sources can be a wellspring of useful information during a competitive analysis, their use shouldn't be limited to that purpose.

The pharmaceutical industry (to cite one example) has a long history of using external research to inform their marketing efforts. They spend a tremendous amount of energy, not to mention dollars, making sure that they have explored every facet of the marketing landscape. They conduct focus groups, online surveys, one-on-one interviews, qualitative and quantitative—just about every possible research methodology known to man. Or woman.

During my tenure as an executive with one of the country's largest pharma ad agencies, I sometimes had the feeling that our clients preferred researching and testing their marketing materials over actually producing them.

Yes, I am being a bit facetious—but I've got to tell you a story that will paint a picture of how external research can be used—and misused.

The following events did really happen.

You would immediately recognize the company—they are one of the best known and largest manufacturers of pharmaceuticals in the world—but there's plenty of water under that bridge, so suffice it to say that we (the company's agency of record for the product) were helping them promote a prominent, lucrative treatment. To gain maximum product uptake, we were pushing the envelope a bit in terms of the claims we were making. This is not unusual—in medical marketing, the agency is often expected to urge the client to push the envelope somewhat, and the manufacturer can accept or reject the attempt.

Pharma companies want to make absolutely sure their messages are going to resonate with prescribing physicians, as well as consumers and, if possible, to what degree. While they need to be somewhat aggressive in their marketing, they have to be careful not to make any claims that will run afoul of the federal regulators at the Food and Drug Administration (FDA) or, for that matter, their own internal legal and regulatory review teams. Also, because the regulatory guidelines can be a moving target, they want to make sure that what's approvable today can still be said in the future—and, hopefully, as far into the future as possible. Consistency of messaging is always a plus, assuming, of course, that the message connects with the audience.

In short, the companies often have to walk a fine line between aggressive messaging and regulatory restrictions.

To locate that sweet spot, they conduct all kinds of research with practicing doctors (and often also with nurses, patients, caregivers, and others), testing various iterations of the messaging. And, when I say messaging, I'm not talking about some words typed on a sheet of printer paper. I'm talking about completely developed, finished-looking mock-ups of the proposed sales materials. Headlines, subheads, pictures, illustrations, charts, references, and all of the other content that the salespeople would need if they were going to use those "messages" to make personal presentations to doctors anywhere in the country. Or, in some cases, to send to the doctors' offices by mail or electronically.

Most of the research that's done to develop those materials is conducted in person, with the pharma company's marketing staff or outside consultants interviewing the doctors, and playing the role of salespeople.

This kind of live research with doctors is a major cottage industry in health care. Pharma holds focus groups, advisory boards, and one-on-one interviews. The demand for doctors to participate is high and the supply is limited. Since the doctors are paid well for their time, research can represent a not insignificant source of income for physicians themselves.

During the years I was in charge of producing the product's promotional material for the agency, our team was tasked with producing new messaging every three months. At the same time, several weeks were needed to prepare the materials for testing. And that testing itself took time. And it inevitably, always led to repeated rounds of revisions.

Yes, it's true. The process of producing the messaging and materials required significantly more time than the three months we were allotted for each round. Often much more. We were perpetually and continuously behind the official timeline, and getting further and further behind for each round of materials, every single day.

The pressure was unrelenting.

The manufacturer was not daunted.

The requirements never changed.

In a fruitless effort to catch up, our entire team worked truly endless hours, week after week, month after month, for a period of years. It felt like we were spinning our wheels deeper and deeper into the mud. Actually, a better analogy would be to say we were trapped in something like F. Scott Fitzgerald's famous description at the end of *The Great Gatsby*:

> *So we beat on, boats against the current, borne back ceaselessly into the past.*

The more we moved forward, the further behind we got.

And yet, face-to-face with the illogical, the unreasonable, the undoable, we persisted. And, after three years of this, because we somehow managed to translate all of that endless input into impactful marketing messages, the product had secured a significantly improved standing in the marketplace.

And not one of us, not a single member of the team, suffered a nervous breakdown.

...as far as I can recall.

Key Takeaways

- Your audience should be a key resource.
- Accurate market data is essential.
- Know yourself and know your market.
- Competitive analysis is like positioning in reverse.

CHAPTER 5

Positioning Step II

The Benefit Ladder

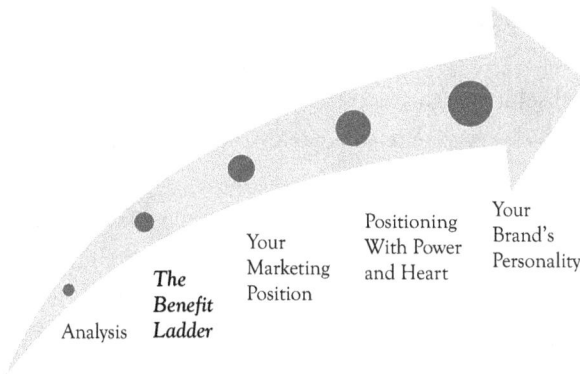

Figure 5.1 Five-step positioning process, highlighting step two

Creating a solidly constructed benefit ladder is the second step in the brand positioning process.

If you're an experienced marketer in the 21st century—and it doesn't matter what you're marketing—you might ask, "Isn't a benefit ladder pretty elementary?" Then you might add, "I'm sure everyone already knows that effective marketing starts with a product's basic attributes and then 'ladders up' through the benefits until you can make an emotional connection with your audience, right?"

I'd reply that a benefit ladder is foundational, like all of the concepts in this book (Figure 5.1). That doesn't make it elementary, in my view.

But another point is worth making. These days almost every marketer seems focused—or even obsessed—with something called "storytelling."

People like to say that, throughout human history, stories have been effective ways to engage people.

Writing for the *Forbes Communications Council*, Maria Hattar said:

> ...for marketing to cut through all the noise and thrive, it should infuse storytelling in everything. Storytelling is powerful because it creates an emotional connection between a company, its products and its customers. Effective storytelling increases engagement between a brand and its audience, which helps drive conversions and, ultimately, revenue growth.... Compelling storytelling lets a brand punch above its weight. [19]

She is absolutely right that stories are very effective at making people feel emotions—and, to reiterate, making the emotional connection is one of the building blocks of an effective marketing position.

So, since most experienced marketers in the 21st century are quite comfortable with the idea that a benefits ladder is a tool that can "ladder up" consumers into an emotionally connected space, then telling your audience a story that leverages that tool to deeply connect them to your offering makes tremendous sense.

But before you can tell your story, you have to know *what the most impactful story is*. And you also need to ensure that the emotion you're communicating is the right one—the one that most effectively, powerfully connects.

To accomplish those tasks, you've got to identify, and then maximize, the features and benefits of your product or service in a systematic and definitive way. That's where the benefits ladder comes in, and it's why it's the next essential step in the positioning process.

So, for those who already employ this step, the following pages are intentionally designed to ensure you're maximizing your efforts. For those new to benefit laddering, this section can make a huge difference in your entire marketing process.

***

The benefit ladder concept dates back to the work of Philip Kotler and his colleague Kevin Lane Keller. Some say Keller originated the concept, but either way, it was developed in response to the sense that marketers at that time were overly focused on products' and services' attributes and features, and were often ignoring the end benefits the product delivered to the consumer.

Richard Czerniawski and Mike Maloney, who have written extensively on the topic, [20] describe a well-made, reliable benefits ladder as having the following characteristics:

- The bottom rungs must be rock-solid—you cannot risk going up to a higher rung if one of the bottom rungs is wobbly or broken.
- All the parts must be made of sturdy material and form into a single unit.
- It must take people up, to some higher place.

"Laddering" helps you go beyond simple features, and encourages you to explore the benefits—from the most basic to the most aspirational.

Benefit ladders urge marketers to stretch themselves, to expand the way they think about—and communicate about—their offerings. Starting at the bottom with the product or service's most basic properties, each rung progresses up to higher-and-higher-level benefits for the customer.

As with so much in marketing theory, over time the benefit ladder has been revised, updated, and "improved." The original ladder attributed to Kotler and Keller was composed of only three "rungs," but other theorists have added more in the years since.

Here is a simple illustration of the original ladder (Table 5.1).

Table 5.1 Benefit ladder, version 1

Emotional End Benefit
Functional Benefit
Attributes

The first rung asks you to identify your offering's attributes and features.

...every single one of them.

Once that's done, you go up to the next level and explore how those properties work. That is, what the product does and what it directly delivers—in other words, its functionality.

A benefit ladder helps build the foundation of success.

I'm going to use an all-electric car (EV) as an example of what this means.

The attributes/properties of an electric car include many things: the basic components (wheels, brakes, chassis, etc.)—and also some things that make it different from a gas-powered vehicle, such as a rechargeable battery and charging port. Also, EVs have a lot fewer moving parts.

What do these various features deliver to the user? Just like a gas-powered car, the electric version gets you from here to there, which is, of course, the primary function of the vehicle, and therefore the primary functional benefit. However, unlike its gas-guzzling cousin's engine, the electric aspect means you don't ever have to visit a gas station. With a simple electric outlet, you can "top off the tank" at home, at will, whenever you need to, probably at a lower cost.

Fewer parts and different parts mean much less maintenance is needed (for one thing, there's no transmission).

Or, if you'd like other examples, remember that a hat is supposed to keep your head warm. Laundry detergent is expected to clean your clothes.

In each example mentioned above, those benefits fit into the second rung in the ladder.

All of these benefits are practical ones, what some experts call "rational" benefits.

In the next rung, we leave the rational world and enter an emotional one. This is a very important place to be, because rung number three considers how the audience feels on an emotional level as they connect with those functional benefits.

Once again, it's important to keep in mind that many marketers—possibly the majority—continue to resist the need to focus on making an emotional connection with their customers (see Saitarli's statement that "80 percent of our clients seem to doubt the strategy—until we deliver results"). The good news is that, as time passes, many successful practitioners have increasingly come to agree that *the emotional space is the space advertising and promotion should try to occupy.*

As we will see as we go forward, the dictum for ad strategists and creators needs to be, "If you engage your audience emotionally, you can truly hook them…potentially for life."

In most cases, it's entirely appropriate that marketers stop when they reach the emotional benefit rung on the ladder. In most cases, that's the real sweet spot, and there's no need to go further (i.e., higher on the ladder).

But it's not where all ladders stop. Some experts have added another, uppermost rung to the model, as follows (Table 5.2).

Table 5.2 Benefit ladder, version 2

Transformational Benefit
Emotional End Benefit
Functional Benefit
Attributes

They continue up into the transformational, or what you might call the "transcendent" realm.

However, the reality is that this added rung—transformational benefits—only applies to a select group of products or services, ones that are genuinely life changing. A cancer or heart drug, a medical or surgical practice, a biomedical device—any and all of these can truly change the course of a life. Few other types of products even aspire to that. Although, if you look at some recent ad campaigns, more than a few apparently believe they can.

Here are two reasons I've included a mention of it:

- First, if your offering can in fact achieve a transformational, life-changing benefit, then your chances for success can be dramatically enhanced. In that case, which is pretty rare, you should certainly do everything you can to reach that rung on the ladder.
- The second reason I've shown this ladder is that such life-changing products or services, when they are found at all, are more commonly found in health care than anywhere else, and health care is the field where I spent much of my professional life.

However, the principles and processes I'm covering are not limited to health care—not at all. They actually can be applied to every business, every product, and every service. That's why, in this book, I'm using the following ladder (Table 5.3), which has important differences compared to the previous ones. It's an adaptation of several expert-developed ladders that have application across a range of fields and categories.

Table 5.3 Benefit ladder, version 3

VERY IMPORTANT EMPTY SPACE
Emotional End Benefit
Functional Benefit
Attributes
Target and Marketing Environment

Let's take a moment to consider the differences between the first two ladders and this third one.

One difference is the addition of the bottommost rung on this third ladder. That rung isn't really a benefit rung at all—it's not even a feature-related rung. Instead, as you see, the box located there says "Target and Marketing Environment," which means that this box serves a completely different purpose. It's a foundational slot that contains all of the background, all of the research, all of the vital preparatory work discussed in the Analysis section of this book.

And, in my opinion, this box of "Target and Marketing Environment"—and in fact all of that foundational work—needs to be recognized as the essential bedrock on which the entire marketing process is built.

Let me say it again:

Every step a marketer takes must rest on a solid, unshakable foundation.

So it's vital to take that bottom, foundational box very seriously.

***

There's another significant difference in this second ladder. You'll notice a box at the very top of the ladder with this strange inscription:

VERY IMPORTANT
EMPTY SPACE

Why is that empty space so important? The thing is, it's not really empty space at all. Far from it.

That space is where your brand's marketing position lives.

Here's the point I'd like you to take away.

All of the work represented by the rungs or boxes in the ladder below that space, all of that effort to identify the attributes, the functional benefits and, most importantly, the emotional benefit, all of that is designed to get you to one result—an effective, enduring marketing position.

Because that's what you are laddering up to achieve in the first place.

I'll talk more about this soon, because that's where all these steps in the process are heading.

***

A key note about benefit ladders: they deliver geometrically increasing impact. So, for example, a functional benefit is an order of magnitude greater than the benefit you can get from your offering's basic attributes. So stepping up to the functional rung can be like entering a completely new world of communication and connection.

Similarly, as consumer neuroscience and other research increasingly tells us, creating an emotional relationship with your consumer is a huge—and extremely powerful—step up from merely presenting a product's functional benefits, regardless of how impressive those benefits might be.

For the vast majority of products and services, as Saitarli points out in the earlier-referenced article, when the key emotional benefit is recognized and then communicated, its resonance with the consumer shows up directly in increased sales. What's more, not only is that resonance likely to dramatically grow your sales, it's also likely to give your connection to your audience real, long-term staying power.

Which might even give you a chance at becoming a timeless brand.

However, it's worth pointing out that functional benefits must be *very* carefully delineated and communicated to make sure that the benefits actually lead the audience—unerringly—to the emotion you want them to feel.

***

To make absolutely sure everyone gets the importance of a well-developed benefit ladder and, particularly, the emotional rung on that ladder, let's quickly go back to that shiny, new, all-electric sport utility vehicle (SUV) someone just left in your driveway.

We've already established that the vehicle has wheels and a battery. Those are basic attributes. But an electric skateboard also has those attributes. Are people likely to pay tens of thousands of dollars for an electric skateboard? Probably not.

Then we added that your EV has functional benefits beyond those attributes, the primary one being transportation. Thing is, an electric skateboard can also move you from here to there. Maybe not as quickly, and it will be unpleasant in a rainstorm…but eventually you can end up where you want to go. And hope someone there has a towel.

So the functional benefits of the e-car have to go beyond mere transportation. And, as we discussed, they do.

However, despite the growing attractiveness (and affordability) of EVs, gas-powered cars still remain a viable option today. They are less expensive on average than EVs and, as of this writing, gas stations are much more readily available than electric car charging stations. Plus, many gas-powered cars have substantially greater range than EVs.

The point is, for a lot of people, the functional benefits of the two vehicles will mostly balance out.

That's why, in the EV example, a marketer would be wise to take things up a rung into the emotional sphere. Because—and you may not know this—even a small, uninspired-looking electric-powered compact can deliver a remarkable emotional jolt. I mean all-electric cars *really* move. They get up to speed effortlessly, and almost instantaneously. Some go from zero to 60 as fast as the fastest street racer. EV drivers get a feeling of power that only a muscle car like a Mustang, BMW, or Porsche can deliver within the internal combustion realm.

If you've spent your life driving a four- or six-cylinder sedan, test drive an EV. You'll be in for a real treat.

While the e-car's acceleration is technically an attribute, it also has substantial functional benefit and, most importantly, it actually moves right up the ladder to supply an emotional end benefit.

Because that emotion, that feeling, that sense of power and confidence you feel when you ease your way effortlessly onto a freeway…well, I wouldn't be surprised if that's what really turned Tesla from a pie-in-the-sky idea into a success story.

Emotional benefits can do that.

Key Takeaways

- Marketing must be built on a solid foundation.
- The benefit ladder is a tool designed to build that foundation.
- The laddering tool can lead to an effective, enduring marketing position.

CHAPTER 6

Positioning Step III

Your Brand's Marketing Position

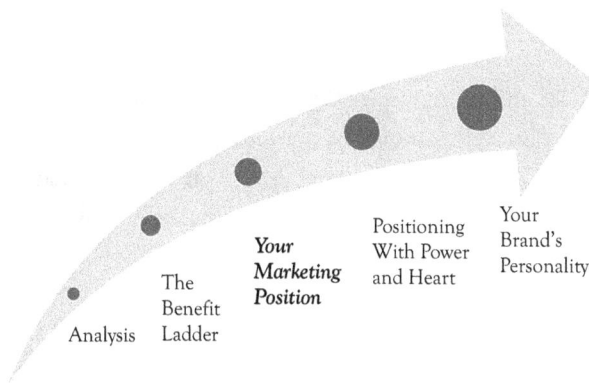

Figure 6.1 Five-step positioning process, highlighting step three

The pivotal step in the brand positioning process is to produce your formal positioning statement, using a structured positioning platform.

Yes, finally, we get to positioning after all the damn prelimi....
Actually, no.

Not at all. And I can't stress this enough. The preceding sections and steps are NOT mere preliminaries. In my experience, they are all truly essential. They represent foundational work that MUST be done. In all cases.

Sorry, there are no exceptions. If you want to be successful.

If you want to be successful, you really, genuinely need to fully understand and faithfully execute the content discussed in the two previous steps in this section. Only then will the marketing position you end up creating get you as far as you can go (Figure 6.1).

Many business books don't emphasize the basic footwork. However, as per the comment from Czerniawski and Maloney (included earlier in a different context), your marketing program's foundation must be rock-solid, and all the parts must be made of sturdy material.

And they must form into a single unit.

And it's vital to repeat that this work must be done with rigor and discipline.

There's no question that those steps take time, especially when done right. And they cost money. (Although, done efficiently, they may cost less than you expect.)

And those are almost always the reasons those foundational steps are not done, or not done thoroughly, rigorously, and with discipline.

That doesn't change the facts. Again, if you want to be as successful as you can be, "your marketing program's foundation must be rock-solid and all the parts be made of sturdy material."

**

By now, you are probably already anxious to see how positioning works in practice. I'll give you a couple of juicy examples of exactly that a little later in the current step. And I'll show how it can work for you.

First, here is the primary tool you will be using.

The Positioning Platform

The positioning platform is the formula you'll follow to create the formal positioning statement. Countless versions of this type of format have proliferated over recent decades, but here's the platform I like to use (Table 6.1).

Basically, our job will be to fill in the slots for each section of the platform for the specific product (or service, or organization) as we build the formal positioning statement.

If you've been working along with the steps so far, you'll be able to easily complete the top two items in the platform. Those are: A summary description of the target audience(s) including the marketing environment (you could cut and paste directly from the benefit ladder); and the competitive framework.

Table 6.1 *Positioning platform format*

Positioning Platform Format	
Target and Marketing Environment	A description of the target audience along with the marketing environment that demonstrates a need for the product
Competitive Framework	For example, are we competing against all consumer beverages, or just carbonated drinks, or just sweetened carbonated drinks?
The Promise	The one thing the product must deliver to the target audience
Reasons to Believe	The facts that support the Promise
Emotional End Benefit	The "so what" to the Promise; how the target audience should feel about the product

Which brings us to the Promise. I've been capitalizing this throughout because the Promise is the beating heart of your positioning statement. The Promise is the *one thing* you will be working to place in the minds of your audience members when they think about your product or service.

The *ONE* thing.

And it's important to be clear about this because, for many organizations, focusing on that one thing is extraordinarily difficult.

So, as much as we may wish it could be, the Promise isn't two things. And it also isn't a single statement with two *really, really* important aspects that really, genuinely, deserve to both be mentioned.

It doesn't mean one thing…and then, "oh, by the way, there's just this one other thing over here…I'm really sorry but I just can't leave it out, I'm sure you understand."

Nope. It means what it says. **ONE thing.**

I've seen many cases where deciding on that one thing has been excruciatingly challenging. You'll even see examples in this book where a given company couldn't quite get itself to achieve that level of discipline.

I've been in too many meetings where clients say "But we're realizing that our offering has so many advantages!" After all, they just spent a huge amount of time and effort on the prior steps. They explored their product's features and benefits, went through a SWOT analysis and a competitive analysis, built a benefit ladder. It was exciting to see so many notable strengths rising to the surface! Now they've got so much to say!

None of that matters. You have to be as disciplined about this as about any other part of the process, and (again) the entire process requires rigorous discipline.

In fact, if you're ever going to be rigorous about anything, this is the time.

Let me put this to you in a different way.

I live in Huntington Beach, California. What a great place to live! The weather is exceptional, there are dozens of great restaurants, beautiful parks, bike trails everywhere, the schools are among the best in the state …I could go on.

However, when, many years ago, Jan Berry and Dean Torrence wrote a famous song about the place, they didn't mention the weather or the restaurants or the parks. They wrote about the one thing that is most notable, most memorable, most worth celebrating—the surf.

The song is *Surf City*. It's a joyous, hard rockin' song, and it's got a great beat, if you like that kind of thing.

Later, when the leading officials of Huntington Beach were trying to decide how to position the city in the minds of the public, I don't know if they developed a formal positioning statement or a formal Promise, but the solution was really a no-brainer.

Surf City.

The *one thing* that really says it all.

So, the question every marketer has to confront, face-to-face, is a simple one. What single thing do you want to celebrate about your offering? What's the one key thing that sets it distinctly apart from every other product or service in its field?

"How," you might ask, "am I going to figure that out?"

The answer is on the summary overview chart provided in Table 6.1. However, I understand that the chart may not make it immediately obvious.

For one thing, getting to the answer does require you to put the cart before the horse for a little while. Because the way to make sure your Promise is the right one is by first exploring and working with the sections of the chart following it. So put the Promise to the side for a little while and focus on:

The reasons to believe and the emotional end benefit.

If you rigorously distill your product's *most convincing* reasons to believe (aka RTBs) and then identify the most viable emotional end benefit, you'll get the right Promise—every single time.

By building a list of ironclad, unchallengeable reasons to believe, and then extracting from the aggregate of those reasons the emotional end benefit that most powerfully connects with your audience (the emotionally powerful "so what" of your Promise), you will find that you're staring at your Promise—the core of your unmistakable, differentiating, marketing position—square in the face.

Let's go back to the BMW example cited earlier in the book. I'll apply it to a modified version of the positioning platform to help visualize how this works (Table 6.2).

Table 6.2 Positioning platform, BMW extrapolation

Competitive Framework	Among automobile manufacturers...
Product Identifier	BMW is the make that gives...
Target Audience	car owners...
The Promise	an exhilarating driving experience...
Reasons to Believe	because it delivers unbeatable performance, technological perfection, luxurious appointments, and a unique approach to automotive design
Emotional End Benefit	**Drivers feel a thrill every time they take the car on the road**

Using this platform grid will consistently deliver a functional, and usually highly effective, positioning statement. And, the more upfront work you do on the earlier steps, the more accurate and effective your statement will be.

***

That's not to say that everything is crystal clear right away. For example, you might be wondering how it's possible to know which facts (i.e., reasons to believe) support the Promise if we don't yet know what the Promise is.

To answer that, I need to explain how I do this part of the process.

First, I go back and thoroughly review all of the analyses accomplished in the previous sections (which, of course, you've already done by this point). To recap, these analyses are as follows:

- Key audiences
- Situation
- Communications

- Competition
- Research
- SWOT
- Benefit ladder

I dig back through all of that information and extract *all* the advantages I've been able to identify. Obviously this includes strengths, opportunities, and benefits, but everything and anything else as well. From that data, I am able to fill in the first two slots in the platform grid back in Table 6.1—audience and competition.

That's where I start, and it's where every positioning platform step needs to begin.

If you've got that done, then you will be looking at a comprehensive list of every single advantage you could come up with.

With that in hand, you'll need to take that lengthy list and cull it down to the essentials. And you'll need to be merciless.

When I say "cull it down to the essentials," here's what I mean. Imagine you were being pressed, and pressed hard, to name the advantages that make your product or service both different *and* better than every other one. Pick those advantages—*and only those*. Bring forward the ones that are most important for your offering. There could be 10, there could be 20. It's unlikely you'll get to 30…and if you're being rigorous, you really won't.

When you have your culled list, step back and take a 30,000-foot view of it. Consider it like you are looking down at a varied landscape from an airplane. What topographic aspects stand out? Where are the highest mountains, the deepest valleys? And then the widest fields, the longest rivers, the largest lakes?

Based on that view, cull the list again. Focus on which advantages stand out the most. Force yourself to make hard choices.

Now, you're getting down to the true essentials, the aspects of your offering that begin to meet the criteria described as "building blocks" back in Part I. To refresh, those criteria are the following:

- Positive value
- Differentiation
- Emotional connection

***

Once you have your very tight, carefully culled list of advantages, take one more really good hard look at it. If you've done all of the preceding steps—and I mean all of them (and would you mind if I reiterate "rigorously, with discipline"?)—you should by now see something—one thing—rise to the surface.

That one thing will be the single aspect of your offering that delivers the greatest **positive value** while strongly **differentiating** you in a way that makes an **emotional connection**.

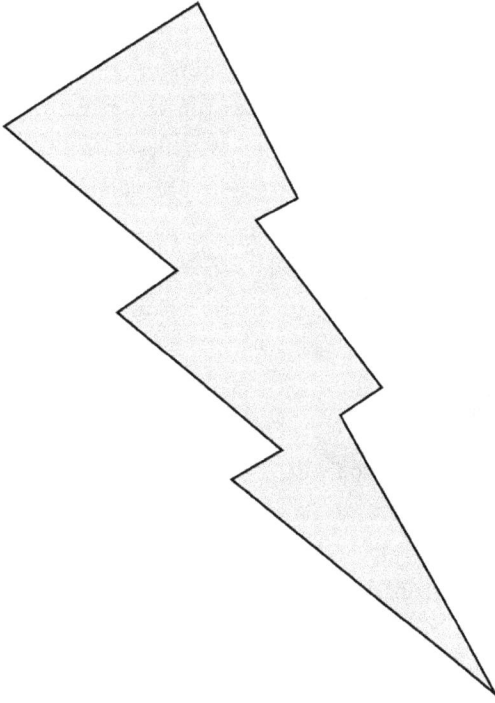

In other words...*your marketing position.*

***

By the way, you may not fully realize it yet, but you were just given the secret to successful marketing.

***

You're welcome.

***

It's important to recognize how central your marketing position will be—not just to your brand and its marketing, but to your entire organization.

You may recall I said earlier that "every single aspect of a product, service, or organization's marketing must be fully and completely aligned with its marketing position."

Now, I'll extend that with a corollary: Every product, service, or organization must *itself also* be fully and completely aligned with its marketing position.

Let's do a thought experiment to emphasize this point.

Imagine you've just been hired to run the marketing department of a company making very high-end, luxury furniture. After you've been there a few weeks, the president of your imaginary company meets with you to share his excitement about some new, advanced technology he recently learned about. He explains that top-quality furniture can now be flawlessly produced utilizing innovative software, automated factories, and even 3D printing. He announces that he and the board have decided to make a major investment in that technology.

Your boss then tasks you with featuring this high-tech concept across all your promotional efforts: the company website, sales materials, social media, and so on. However, the available data shows that the segment of the luxury furniture market you serve prefers a very traditional approach to manufacture. Your customers care about craftsmanship and personal, individualized attention to detail. You've also seen that your direct competitors' promotional campaigns are filled with charming, homey vignettes about the experienced artisans who painstakingly build each chair and table by hand.

The personal touch is what consumers are seeking in your segment. If you begin highlighting that your products are churned out by an automated, robotic process, customers are likely to turn elsewhere.

Yet your boss insists.

What to do?

Let's go back to Theodore Levitt's point from Chapter 3. He says, in marketing, it's not about the product, it's about the offering.

In this case, the company's offering will soon include a primary aspect that is at odds with customers' desires.

You'll have quite a challenging choice in this situation. You might be able to use the new production method to differentiate from the competition, adapting your positioning to match the new reality—and hope you can find enough customers who find it attractive. A risky proposition at best. Or, you can try to gloss over the truth (undoubtedly incurring the wrath of your higher-ups) and build a Promise and a marketing position that is not supported by viable reasons to believe. In that case, your positioning statement will have an unavoidable defect, even though the product you produce may be repeatably perfect.

As a talented marketer, you'll probably be able to devise another solution. But the point of this exercise is not to solve this dilemma. Instead the point is to show how essential it is to ensure that your organization, or at least the key aspects of it, are fully aligned with your marketing position. When you have a disconnect like this one, matching the factual basis of your offering to a strong, commercially viable position is difficult, if not impossible. If you conduct a SWOT analysis, you will find your weaknesses inevitably overwhelming your strengths. Your threats will be greater than your opportunities. And aligning your Promise to your reasons to believe may simply not be feasible.

That's why it's so important for every organization and every offering to be consistently and fully aligned with its marketing position. Otherwise, its basic marketing foundation is shaky at best.

I learned this firsthand through personal experience. I've worked with more than one medical practice offering new, highly advanced procedures that expected change-adverse communities to enthusiastically buy into the new, cutting-edge approach. And I've helped companies who had to rethink and retool their entire approach to their market because consumers changed their buying habits. And there are many other examples.

In every case, the closer the alignment between offering and marketing position, the greater was the chance for success.

***

The next two chapters feature practical examples of positioning and are taken from my own career.

Key Takeaways

- The positioning platform is used to create your positioning statement.
- Your Promise is the one thing you'll place in your audience's minds.
- Combine your RTBs and emotional end benefit to produce your Promise.
- Ideally, every aspect of your organization should be aligned with your marketing position.

CHAPTER 7

Positioning Example #1

Promoting "Pharma Product X"

This example examines a few possible marketing positions to arrive at the strongest option.

This chapter will focus on the pharmaceutical space and explore a range of possible positioning platforms for a specific offering.

Let's call it Product X and say it was designed to treat Condition Y. The lack of specifics won't matter in this case; in fact, that will help to generalize the example.

For background, Product X was in the early, prelaunch strategy phase when the positioning was done. We will look at the situation from a few angles so you can see the types of choices and challenges you may face when you do this for your brand.

During the situational analysis, several key facts quickly rose to the surface:

- Condition Y resulted from a gene mutation that caused an error affecting metabolism.
- Condition Y negatively and dramatically affected patients' quality of life, causing major life issues.
- If left untreated, the condition often resulted in progressive neurological impairment.
- Before the introduction of Product X, **there was no medication-based treatment** for Condition Y.

- The only previously available approach included
  - A highly restrictive diet
  - Frequent check-ins with physicians and dietitians
  - And, again, no treatment with medication.

In contrast, Product X was:

- The first medication-based approach to Condition Y.
- A scientifically advanced treatment with a unique mechanism of action.
  * HOWEVER * While the medication was FDA approved, no long-term studies had been done and both patients and physicians considered the treatment to be novel and feared possible long-term risks.
- Product X had been studied in high-quality clinical trials that demonstrated positive efficacy with minimal side effects.
  * HOWEVER * When side effects did occur, they were serious; also, therapeutic delivery was intravenous, which is always an obstacle to patient uptake.

Market research showed that the standard, non-medicine-based treatment model negatively impacted patients. The lack of viable medication left patients feeling distraught and ignored and physicians also were unhappy, feeling helpless and frustrated at the lack of a medicinal option. At the same time, patients' fears and physicians' concerns about possible long-term risks from the new treatment could not be ignored.

Four Positioning Options

The first positioning option focuses on the patients' sense of being neglected by the medical industry.

In this first example (Table 7.1), you'll notice a few things that each one of these will all have in common:

- The Target and Marketing Environment can be—and needs to be—presented as succinctly as possible.
- The first four sections are integrally linked, which is shown by the use of ellipses.

- The three middle sections, taken as a group, emerge from the platform to become the formal positioning statement.
- The RTBs also need to be stated as briefly as possible.
- The emotional benefit is what the entire positioning process is intended to accomplish.

Table 7.1 *Positioning platform, pharma option 1*

Position #1	
Target and Marketing Environment	For patients who have tried the limited available options, and have felt alone and unsupported in their battle as they continue to experience Condition Y effects…
Competitive Framework	Product X is the medical therapy…
Product Promise	…that answers these patients' needs…
Reasons to Believe	…because it is the first therapy to provide clinical efficacy as well as limited side effects
Emotional End Benefit	Patients feel grateful that their appeals have been heard and responded to

In this version, it may at first glance appear that the position could be boiled down to "the product is safe and effective." And, looking at that, you could certainly be excused for responding, "Wait a minute, that sounds like two things! Didn't you say that a position must be the *one thing* you will be working to implant in the minds of your audience?"

I did say that, multiple times. The thing is, in this case, what looks like two things is actually just two sides of a single coin.

In the medical field, no product can be marketed if it isn't safe, and safety must be proven by clinical trials and then certified by the FDA. So safety, while it must be proven and must be clearly stated, is a requirement, not a benefit. It is a strict, unalterable stipulation and must be achieved. The product simply can't be legally marketed unless it is proven safe. (Note: In this case, the safety had been proven through short-term clinical trials. Its long-term safety remained unknown.)

And while efficacy must also be proven in order to receive FDA approval, there are different types and degrees of efficacy. For example, showing that a pain medication is effective would be quite different than showing that a drug reduces bad cholesterol, or that another product eases the symptoms of allergic rhinitis.

In this case, Product X's efficacy is game changing. No prior approach was able to achieve a level of effectiveness that was even comparable. So, in this case, "safe and effective" amounts to the product's single Promise.

And, in this case, it really is the whole ballgame.

That's why it's important to look at the Promise:

"Answers these patients' need."

I think we can agree that the Promise (in this version) is well aligned with the marketing situation as described in the Target and Marketing Environment block. Patients are seeking a response that makes them feel less alone and unsupported, and, by providing unprecedented efficacy (with safety), Product X "answers the need."

There is an emotional end benefit—because the product is available, patients will feel supported with their medical need finally being met.

That's all fine, and this option could be a viable marketing position. But is it the strongest one we can come up with?

Let's start looking at the others and see (Table 7.2).

Table 7.2 Positioning platform, pharma option 2

Position #2	
Target and Marketing Environment	For patients who continue to suffer from Condition Y despite available care; are frustrated by disruptions to their lives caused by the condition; and fear the condition's long-term effects…
Competitive Framework	Product X is the medical therapy…
Product Promise	…that empowers patients to regain control of their lives…
Reasons to Believe	…because it is the first therapy to provide clinical efficacy as well as limited side effects
Emotional End Benefit	Patients feel renewed confidence in their ability to face the future

Right from the start, this is a noticeably different approach. Instead of feeling alone and unsupported as stated in option #1, we are now acknowledging that patients are suffering, and that they are also frustrated and fearful.

Yes, Position #1 is correct that it's hard to be alone, and it acknowledges that feeling unsupported can make that worse. But those feelings seem minor when compared to real physical suffering—significant discomfort, possibly even serious pain. Add the challenges of living with a disruptive condition and the specter of long-term disability, and a medication that can resolve those issues could be life-changing.

And yet, here the Promise—while viable— doesn't seem to maximize that value. Focused on regaining control, it doesn't mention alleviating patients' suffering or resolving the other issues.

Similarly, the emotional benefit is all about confidence and hope. Again, those are important emotions, but the benefits statement doesn't seem to fully appreciate the far-reaching, major improvement Product X can produce in the patient's moment-by-moment, day-to-day quality of life.

For me, neither of these first two marketing options really hits the mark. So let's move on to the next one (Table 7.3) and see where it takes us.

Table 7.3 Positioning platform, pharma option 3

Position #3	
Target and Marketing Environment	For patients who continue to suffer from Condition Y and have been disappointed by the ineffectiveness of current treatment approaches…
Competitive Framework	Product X is the medical therapy…
Product Promise	…that outsmarts Condition Y…
Reasons to Believe	…because it offers the first medication-based, scientifically advanced treatment approach against Condition A
Emotional End Benefit	Patients feel empowered and relieved to have science on their side at last

Did you feel the difference when you read that? It starts with a shift within the Target and Marketing Environment block. While this version does contain elements from the ones in options 1 and 2, the major component of the mindset now is disappointment instead of loneliness or frustration.

And then, when we get to the Promise, we begin to see that we're truly in a completely different sphere.

In this case, we see the Promise talking about "smarts." We might wonder why. After all, the positioning platform shows that a marketing position should lead to an emotional end benefit.

And that idea is supported by what we've already seen from various sources and experts about the power of emotion in marketing.

So, yes, it's great to have intelligence and science on our side when faced with a debilitating disease. But "smarts" is about rational thought, which is the polar opposite of emotional content.

And, when we arrive at the emotional benefit block, we see that, in fact, the emotional payoff is not very strong. Sure, it's great to feel empowered and relieved, but that doesn't really measure up to alleviating loneliness or ending frustration.

Having spent many years in science-based marketing, I've seen how positions based on hard scientific facts often leave their audiences cold. While many health care and pharmaceutical products adopt that kind of approach, those products typically don't connect very well on an emotional level.

The reason for this isn't complicated. While a scientific story can certainly have value, science is, by definition, dispassionate and impersonal. And so it's hardly surprising that science-based marketing positions struggle when it comes to a powerful emotional end benefit.

I strongly believe that success in marketing is tied directly to making the connection to the audience as personal and passionate as it can be.

We've now examined three positioning options and analyzed their strengths and weaknesses. While it's possible to make a case for each one, for my money, none of them have the vital power and undeniable emotional impact we should expect from a medication like Product X—one that can change people's lives.

And so I turn my gaze hopefully forward to option #4 (Table 7.4).

Table 7.4 Positioning platform, pharma option 4

Position #4	
Target and Marketing Environment	For patients who continue to suffer from Condition Y despite making use of currently available care; are frustrated by disruptions to their lives; and fear the condition's long-term effects...
Competitive Framework	Product X is the medical therapy...
Product Promise	...that gives patients a new chance at life...
Reasons to Believe	...because it is the first efficacious medication with limited side effects that's available to patients who have Condition Y.
Emotional End Benefit	Patients feel relieved that they can get back to a normal, enjoyable life and a bright future

The Target and Marketing Environment block is similar to previous ones. But take a good look at that Promise:

"A new chance at life."

Now, *that's* a strong Promise! That's optimism! There's genuine hope! It's like getting the opportunity to breathe fresh air again. And that Promise is strongly supported by unarguable reasons to believe. So it's not surprising that, when we get to the emotional payoff, we see that it only underscores the Promise's strength, because it includes powerful, uplifting sentiments: relief, normality, and enjoyment, not to mention a bright future.

What more can someone who's been suffering and frustrated ask for than a chance to regain their normal life, and to experience the potentially lifelong relief that can flow from that?

Another important thing to note in this option is how seamlessly the middle three sections work together to form a clear, robust positioning statement.

Plus, the statement includes all three of the building blocks of positioning:

1. Positive value: An efficacious medication with limited side effects.
2. Differentiation: The first medication available to treat Condition Y.
3. Emotional connection: Ability to experience a normal, enjoyable life and a bright future.

Keep all of that in mind, then think for a moment about what a competitor would have to do to undermine or attack Product X, assuming our product successfully connects this position to its audience. How would the competing company go about it?

They would have an awfully tough time, wouldn't they?

That has to help the marketing team at Product X sleep well at night, I would think.

Key Takeaways

- To create the most effective positioning platform, consider a range of options.
- A strong emotional end benefit typically results in a robust positioning statement.
- A powerful Promise is essential for a solid marketing position.

CHAPTER 8

Positioning Example #2

Repositioning "Niche Nutrition, Inc."

This example demonstrates how positioning-based marketing can overcome major marketing—and organizational—challenges.

Within the past few years, I began working with a team helping a vitamin and nutritional supplement manufacturer/distributor that I'll call "Niche Nutrition, Inc." That fictitious name is intended to be descriptive—while the company was well-established as a manufacturer of high-quality natural vitamins, it had been only serving a small slice of the market, a niche that was based on the ethnicity of the company's management.

They had been successful connecting with that ethnic group, but any attempts to expand out of their niche had borne little fruit. And now the company's growth had slowed substantially and the effectiveness of its digital efforts, including e-commerce, was decreasing.

I was working with an innovative agency team and we immediately dove in and began an in-depth assessment. It quickly became clear that, if Niche was ever going to broaden its market, it would need to take a hard look at its overall situation, particularly its marketing position.

Implementing the Analysis

We started with a survey of Niche's marketing situation and brand communications. Our review included an examination of the company's overarching and specific marketing strategies and tactics, including positioning, key audiences, and range of marketing activities. Given that the company's primary source of income was its e-commerce website, we put great focus on digital marketing efforts.

We studied key company and brand personality traits and marketing characteristics, conducted an audience analysis, product capability analysis, competitive analysis, and SWOT analysis, and also provided a sophisticated, in-depth audit of digital analytics. We also did a tactical review, with a focus on messaging and brand voice, graphic design, search engine optimization (SEO), keywords, pay-per-click, and search engine marketing, among other aspects.

Progressing Through the Process

With the research done, a few conclusions became inescapable: Niche need to reposition its primary product line, and also to reconceptualize the overall brand personality. Moreover, it became clear that the company would benefit from certain organizational changes.

For the purpose of this chapter, I'll be focusing on the positioning process; however, it's important to note that the leadership's recognition of the need for repositioning had a cascade effect. Initially, it helped them understand an overhaul of their website experience, along with the company's entire digital content structure, was required. Next, they took a step back and looked at their entire business model through the lens of their new position and began making changes everywhere that was practical.

They were willing to make wide-ranging changes because they began to see that positioning is the centerpiece of their entire business. They grasped that the effects of repositioning can be expected to reach beyond marketing—that it can impact every aspect of an organization's existence.

In this case, repositioning changed the company's social marketing efforts; upgraded its blog content and branded video offerings; and revised its branding, brand identity, and packaging. In addition, it led the company to rethink aspects of product development, to restructure its sales efforts, and to consider a new approach to distribution, among other things.

Positioning Steps

Once Niche's leadership recognized and accepted the pivotal nature of positioning, the agency team and I began moving through the systematic process, step by step. During the initial research, we'd learned about the company's strengths and opportunities; and we'd clarified where best to focus our efforts—we were identifying the key reasons to believe. A clear and differentiating marketing position vis-à-vis the competition began to emerge.

We took the following steps to identify a strong marketing position for Niche:

1. Listed the reasons to believe (see the following);
2. Distilled the RTBs until they codified the company's ideal value proposition;
3. Isolated the essence of what makes Niche and its products special and distinct;
4. Summarized the differentiation and the value in a bedrock marketing position statement;
5. Achieved agreement from Niche's leadership to fully implement the new position.

To give you a better sense of what an RTB list looks like, I'm providing the finalized (and somewhat summarized) list of reasons we used:

1. Niche is managed by medically trained and highly credentialed physicians and scientists.
2. The company takes a holistic and science-based approach that leverages the company's unusually high level of medical and scientific expertise and experience.
3. Niche has created high-quality supplements that are provably the purest in the marketplace.
4. Niche offers a comprehensive line of nutritional supplements that are certified pure by three licensed, independent outside agencies.
5. Niche's products only use natural ingredients.
6. All Niche products meet stringent FDA requirements, good marketing practices (GMP), and other recognized scientific and manufacturing standards.
7. Niche's products have been rated higher for potency and stability (within shelf-life limitations) than any competitors' product lines.

Again, this list has been shortened for this book, but retains all of the key information we used to create the company's marketing position statement.

Here's the way it would work within the positioning platform grid (Table 8.1).

Table 8.1 *Positioning platform, Niche Nutrition*

Target and Marketing Environment	For consumers who are seeking a comprehensive line of high-quality nutritional supplements...
Competitive Framework	Niche is the vitamin and supplement manufacturer/ distributor...
Product Promise	...that delivers a comprehensive line of superior, natural products...
Reasons to Believe	...because it is managed by medically trained and highly credentialed physicians and scientists; takes a holistic and science-based approach; only offers supplements that are certified pure by three licensed, independent outside agencies; and which are highly rated for potency and stability
Emotional End Benefit	Patients are excited to find a source for nutritional products that they can trust

And here is the resulting summary statement:

Niche Nutrition supplies scientifically developed, certified-pure products to consumers who need to trust the nutritional efficacy of the vitamins and supplements that they buy.

And, once again, the statement includes all three of the building blocks of positioning:

1. Positive value;
2. Differentiation: Scientifically developed, certified-pure products;
3. Emotional connection: A sense of trust in the products' nutritional efficacy.

Massaging the Messaging

While messaging is actually an aspect of a brand's personality and not, strictly speaking, part of the positioning process, it will help for you to see how a brand's positioning can play out in the messaging presented to the end user. It's interesting to note that, when we tested and retested a range of messages based on the positioning statement shown previously, two things became clear.

First, purity was a key selling point. It was particularly important to the young mothers who comprised the company's primary consumer audience.

Second, while the company's preexisting and long-standing emphasis on science was consistent with the "purity" idea, it actually hid a vital characteristic—one that aligned better with purity and contained much more emotional content.

That characteristic was honesty.

Why? Most consumers see scientists as fact-based thinkers and seekers after truth, both positive attributes. However, scientists are also seen as cold and dispassionate. As we've discussed, those are not characteristics likely to create an emotional bond.

However, when the company's scientific capabilities were seen through the lens of honesty, the sense of coldness receded and the scientists' passion for (and commitment to) truth rose to the surface. This passion for truth and honesty underscored the power of purity in a way that no other terminology was able to do in our testing—and it engendered the sense of trust we already knew was the emotional benefit central to the marketing position.

These factors, when processed in context of the new positioning statement, led to a new Niche theme line. As I've mentioned earlier, a positioning statement is for internal use, and that language is never intended for public consumption. The company's theme line was designed to simplify the positioning and begin to create a brand story that would make an emotional connection to a broader consumer audience, while also keeping current customers in mind.

The new theme is:

Niche Nutrition. Honestly Pure.

Going forward...*all aspects of every communication*...including copy and design and sales messaging, began working in unison to leverage the idea that consumers could trust the company's commitment to honest purity.

In short, through our positioning process and follow-on messaging efforts, we had put our finger on the company's emotional end benefit.

Were our efforts successful? After implementing our process, Niche Nutrition quickly transformed from a niche company into one with increasingly broad appeal. In fact, less than three years later, it was sold to a nationally known nutritional company, resulting in a substantial profit for Niche's ownership.

***

The examples given for Product X and Niche Nutrition demonstrate, in some depth, the type of approaches and the kind of thinking required to deliver a powerful marketing position for a given product. Really, for any given product or service. In fact, if you take the time to apply the principles employed in those examples, it should be obvious that those principles—and the process—can be easily transferred to any product, any service, and any organization. Really, to any brand.

Key Takeaways

- The market positioning process can have wide-ranging effects, including organizational change.
- The positioning statement codifies the essence of the offering.
- A brand's position provides the basis for messaging and follow-on communications.

CHAPTER 9

Positioning Step IV

Brand Positioning With Power; Marketing With Heart

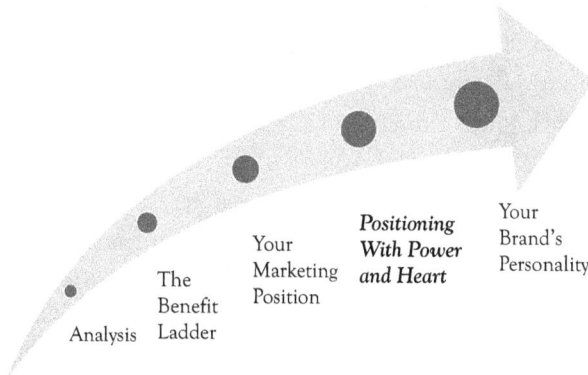

Figure 9.1 Five-step positioning process, highlighting step four

It's increasingly clear that emotional connection is an essential build-ing block in an effective positioning process.

What supplies the power in "brand positioning with power?"

Great question. And, by now, you already know the answer.

Throughout this book, I've been making the case that emotion is the key to successful marketing. That emotion plays a pivotal role in positioning your brand in the marketplace (Figure 9.1).

For decades, many, if not most, corporations' advertising and marketing communications were intentionally impersonal. They featured pleasant, yet one-dimensional, images that were accompanied by formal, businesslike and flatly unemotional copy.

More recently, awareness of the value of emotional marketing content has grown significantly. It has increased to the extent that an emphasis on emotion, even passion, has become a central aspect of countless advertising and promotional campaigns. The reasons for this are many—but the most important may be that there's a solid scientific basis for this approach. To reiterate what Dr. Peter Noel Murray wrote in *Psychology Today*:

> Functional magnetic resonance imaging (fMRI) shows that when evaluating brands, consumers primarily use emotions (personal feelings and experiences), rather than information (brand attributes, features, and facts).
>
> Studies show that positive emotions toward a brand have a far greater influence on consumer loyalty than trust and other judgments, which are based on a brand's attributes. [14]

When we explored benefit ladders and positioning platforms, we saw that making an emotional connection is fundamental and pivotal for effective use of both of those tools. And, in turn, those two tools are essential aspects of the process of positioning a brand with power, which supports my theme that emotional resonance is fundamental and pivotal to the successful marketing that positioning is designed to achieve.

These facts have significant implications. Taken together, they demonstrate the essential message of this book. That message, concisely stated, is as follows:

The overriding task for today's marketers is to employ the positioning process to ensure that their brand reaches *beyond* the mind—and into the heart.

So let's stop there. Because that assertion raises what may potentially be a very controversial question:

Were Ries and Trout actually wrong, right from the start?

***

That's quite a question. What would make me ask that question?

The answer is based in the original (and quite famous) definition of positioning Ries and Trout offered in their book from 1981. Here, again, is how they describe positioning:

*Positioning is not what you do to a product. Positioning is what you do to the mind of the prospect. That is, you position (place) the product **in the mind** of the potential buyer.*

They put the entire weight of the positioning process on establishing a hold on the mind. In a later, updated work called *The New Positioning*, Jack Trout reiterates the original emphasis he and Ries put on a rational, not emotional connection, saying: "The ultimate marketing battleground is the mind." [21]

Yet, an increasing number of experts and a growing volume of scientific data of the kind that is offered earlier in this book shows that, when evaluating brands, consumers primarily use emotions rather than what the rational mind is focused on—objective information.

So it's essential to remember that, when we worked through the benefit ladder, we found that:

Rung number three is focused on how the audience feels on an emotional level as they connect with those functional benefits.

As you'll recall, rung number three is crucial to the creation of a functioning benefit ladder; and a functioning benefit ladder is crucial to effective positioning; and, of course, effective positioning underlies the success of the entire marketing effort.

The reality is that, whenever we looked in detail at specific positioning examples, we saw—over and over again—how absolutely central emotional content was to marketing success. We saw, in fact, that arriving at a strong emotional end benefit was the real point of the entire positioning platform.

***

Now I can almost hear you say, "Hey…hold on now…wait just one minute. At the beginning of this book, didn't you say, 'Al Ries and Jack Trout [are] the innovators who birthed the idea of market positioning?' That their insights were revolutionary?"

***

Of course they did. And of course they were. Ries and Trout are the innovators. They developed the remarkable concept, and they were brilliant at it. And I'm not saying they were completely wrong.

Quite the contrary. They were *completely correct* that placing your product in the mind of the consumer is essential. You will get absolutely nowhere if you don't.

However, over the course of my career, it's become increasingly clear that focusing on the mind is only one part of the marketer's task. Of your task.

The second part—maybe not more important, but certainly equally vital—is to make an emotional connection between your product and the consumer's heart.

In fact, this entire book has been designed to gradually, and I hope convincingly, bring you, the reader, step by step to this moment. My goal was to introduce the incremental understanding that, in fact, Ries and Trout—great as they are, truly brilliant as they've consistently been— well, maybe they simply didn't consider the emotional aspect. Or maybe they didn't realize its value as a separate and distinct aspect of "the mind." Or possibly, the overall environment in marketing and advertising at the time caused them to discount it.

Whatever their reason might have been, the fact is that now, decades after Ries and Trout published their groundbreaking work, it's time for a new kind of thinking about positioning, the kind that this book provides. While I believe the basic concept Ries and Trout created remains the central pillar in modern marketing, I'm also convinced that it's time to add a new dimension to the foundation they built.

It's time to broaden the definition of positioning beyond the mind, and into the heart.

The good news is that the importance of this idea has in fact been slowly rising in the consciousness of marketers across the globe, and that is very encouraging indeed. But my cousin, friend, and frequent writing partner, the man who is the first person I thank in the acknowledgments for this book… well…Ed Shankman may have gotten there before most of the rest.

Here's what he recently said to me, making a statement that beautifully capsulizes this new thinking. The way he phrased his view of the matter was powerful in its simplicity. He said:

Make a positive emotional connection, and you'll make the sale. Deepen the connection, and you'll keep making sale after sale after sale.

I couldn't agree more. Do those things, and you may well have the consumer hooked.

For life.

***

In fact, I believe the case for this approach is ironclad. How ironclad? I'll summarize and reinforce it quickly here, and you can decide for yourself.

Here are the "heart-related" points made during the course of this book:

1. The purpose of a benefit ladder is to help the consumer learn enough and care enough about your offering that they begin to form an emotional connection with it.
2. The power of the emotional connection is confirmed by experts as well as by substantial (and ever-increasing amounts of) scientific data.
3. Use of the positioning platform demonstrates that a key justification for creating a marketing position is to identify (and then utilize) the emotional end benefit that connects with consumers.
4. The emotional end benefit is the "so what" to your Promise. It's how you want your customers to feel about your brand, and how your brand connects to their hearts.
5. Your efforts in positioning (and branding) should be focused on both securing a place in consumers' minds, and also in making a personal and heart-felt connection with your audience that will form a lasting emotional bond.

Again, these points are strongly supported by an increasing number of experts, reams of research, and an emerging, entirely new field in neuroscience. And I'll provide additional examples of how this works in practice, in the coming pages.

So let's emphasize this crucial aspect: Yes, please, absolutely do what Ries and Trout advise. Place your product directly and firmly in the minds of your prospects.

And appeal to their hearts.

Because that's what will give your brand's position its power.

***

> *Well, I'm on my way. I don't know where I'm going, but I'm on my way...*
> —Paul Simon

As Paul Simon humorously suggests in *Me and Julio Down in the Schoolyard*, people need to know where they're going if they're ever going to get there. This is equally true of companies and brands. And, once they set that goal, they need to decide how to get from here to there; what road to take.

That decision could also be called "setting their strategy."

At this point, we've explored the first four steps in the positioning process and the word "strategy" has come up every so often. But we really haven't paid the topic much attention.

You'd be right to ask, "Why not? Strategy is a significant part of marketing, isn't it?"

It certainly is. Particularly in a book about positioning, we need to consider how marketing strategy fits into the overall positioning picture. For example, is it integral to positioning, or is it separate and distinct? Should the strategy be developed before going through the positioning process? After? During?

These are all key considerations. And I've been holding back on this until now for a reason.

The truth is, talking about strategy makes some folks start to squirm. One reason is that the whole topic is remarkably nebulous.

Consider simply trying to come up with a definition. You'll recall, when we tried to define positioning, that no consensus definition exists. In that case, at least we have Ries and Trout's original formulation to rely on.

No such benchmark exists for strategy—none at all. Quite the contrary. By one count, there are nearly 400,000 separate definitions of the word listed in Google.

So let's see what Philip Kotler, who many consider the father of the field, says on the topic. He describes marketing strategy as: "The basic approach that the business unit will use to attain its goals…[Strategy is] a set of objectives, policies, and rules that serve as guidelines in a certain period of time for a company's marketing activity."[22]

In other words, he's saying that adopting a strategy means deciding on a directional mindset (the road to take, or the "basic approach") and then enforcing that mindset (or following that road) using policies and guidelines—that is, the rules of the road.

Kotler's approach makes a lot of sense. However, if you look at Kotler's statement carefully, it's clear that something is lurking behind his formulation—there's an implied, yet quite important, prior step.

Goals first have to be set. In other words. . . .

You have to decide where you want to go if you're ever going to get there.

Or, as Bryan W. Barry puts it, strategy is "The process of determining what your organization intends to accomplish, and how you direct the organization…toward accomplishing these goals." [23]

Only with a clear destination in mind can you develop an effective strategy.

We all need a goal for our efforts, and once we've set our goal, we need to figure out how to achieve it. What direction are we heading? What's the best path to take?

***

Taking all this into account, here's the definition of strategy I use in my marketing work:

Your strategy is the evidence-based, foundational approach and mindset most likely to guide you and your product from *where you are* to *where you want to go.*

I need to emphasize a couple of points from that definition. First, it's vital that the entire endeavor must be evidence-based. Despite the fact that hardly anyone can agree on how to define strategy, there is actually a broad consensus that strategies must be based on solid evidence—on hard data, thoroughly analyzed. That's the first consideration in my definition, and it is fully consistent with the steps in the positioning process I've described in this book.

Second, my version emphasizes the foundational nature of strategy development. This is crucial. Because, once you adopt a mindset—that is, once you choose the road you're going to take and commit to that approach, to your strategy—well, everything else should follow—really, must follow—from that original, foundational choice.

AND I MEAN *EVERYTHING.*

Reading this, maybe you'll say, "Okay, I can accept that as a working definition." But then you would be within your rights to add, "Based on that, go ahead and tell me how to choose and develop an effective strategy."

Truly, a reasonable request.

***

However, before I reply, it's vital to be clear about one thing. Many marketers—even the most highly trained MBAs—often conflate strategic processes with tactical planning. I encourage you to take a look at a range of marketing plans; or search online for "strategic planning steps"; and you'll see a surprisingly frequent emphasis on tactics. You'll see less attention given to developing a **"foundational approach and mindset."**

I've been part of countless kickoff meetings, beginning big, important, and expensive new marketing efforts—meetings that should have begun with a deep dive into the strategic foundation of the entire enterprise—and, instead, seen them turn almost entirely into tactical discussions.

That is a **foundational** mistake.

***

Now, let's get back to that great request:

"Tell me how to choose and develop an effective strategy."

The truth is that the five steps we're going through *are what you need* for the task.

Exactly what you need.

To be as clear as possible, marketing strategy development is a by-product of the positioning process. If you are following the steps detailed in these pages, your marketing strategy—an effective marketing strategy—will emerge. *Organically.*

When you've completed these steps, you will find that you've been gifted an effective strategy. You will have a fully formed, strategically designed opportunity to create a successful brand.

***

I'm aware that the way strategy emerges organically from the positioning process is not self-evident. So, to show how this works, here are a couple of 30,000-foot snapshots of concrete examples.

Imagine this scenario: You conduct a situation analysis that shows your company has massive resources and only minimal competition (wouldn't that be great?). Relying on that analysis and following the subsequent steps in the positioning process, you realize that, in your field, you can assert dominant leadership, and become the "eight-hundred-pound gorilla." That is the key to your marketing position (not your marketing statement, as we've previously discussed).

Amazon has become a classic example of this market position, though in their case they have asserted a position of dominance in multiple fields.

Based on that marketing position, your strategy then is inevitable: You take the path of the category leader. What mindset did Amazon adopt when it recognized it was dominating online shopping? It asserted its leadership in every way it could. Why did it do this? Because that strategy fit the situation.

And that strategy emerged organically from its marketing position.

Conversely, Amazon wouldn't have, couldn't have, adopted that strategy when it was a smaller, struggling company. Because it didn't yet fit the situation. Back then, a marketing position of dominant leadership would have been entirely aspirational.

I realize that I've asked you to create an imaginary situation and, even if you're a dominant company, you're not likely to be Amazon. But if your imaginary company has powerful resources and minimal competition, dominant leadership can become the key to your marketing position and it can be your foundational approach. It's the mindset you—and everyone else in your company—can take with you to work every day.

The decisions that you make with that mindset will be *very* different than the ones you would be making if your resources were limited and competition was fierce. If you find yourself in a dominant situation, everything you do—everything—will flow from that overall strategic approach. Including the way you go about creating strong emotional bonds with your customers.

For example, take a look at the Amazon smile logo. That should tell you a lot about how they do business.

Now let's consider the opposite scenario. This time, imagine that, even though it has been around for a while, your company hasn't successfully maximized its resources. Because of its struggles, you and the rest of the leadership face obstacles everywhere you turn. Also, the competition is a genuine threat.

In this case, you face a very different situation, so your approach will also have to be dramatically different. As you go through the positioning process, you might determine that the best marketing position at this point in your company's life cycle would be to refocus as a niche business. Or maybe you'll decide to focus your positioning around the one or two most successful products in your line.

Scenario one is very different from scenario two. And your strategy will therefore be *very* different, based on the situation you are facing and the marketing position you adopt. However, whatever marketing position best fits your situation, your strategy will inevitably and organically emerge from it.

> A strong marketing position leads to effective strategy.

It goes without saying that there are countless other scenarios, and each can branch into a wide range of positions, and strategic approaches.

However, whichever position you choose to adopt, that choice will determine your strategy...what I've also called "your approach" or "mindset."

The direction you take.

Whatever you call it, it will emerge directly and organically from your market positioning process.

Then, *that* will inevitably lead to the various ways your brand will interact with your market, in tactics such as your messaging and promotional campaigns.

Key Takeaways

- Emotional connection provides the power to your marketing position.
- Marketers need to ensure that their brand reaches beyond the mind and into the heart.
- Your marketing strategy will emerge organically from your brand's position.

CHAPTER 10

Positioning Step V

Brand Personality and a Timeless Brand

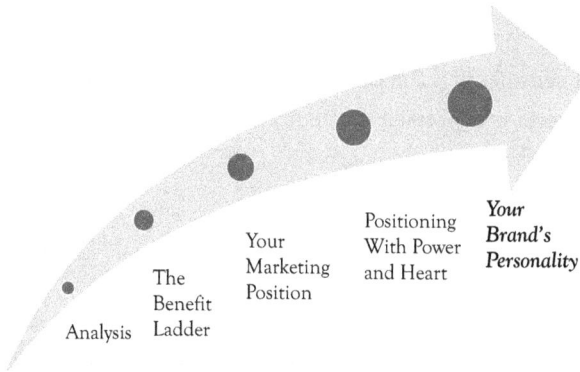

Figure 10.1 Five-step positioning process, highlighting step five

Developing a differentiating marketing position leads directly to implementing a unique brand personality.

Decades after Ries and Trout made their mark, Jennifer Aaker was credited with developing the brand personality concept (Figure 10.1). Here's an adaptation of Aaker's approach, as shown in Figure 10.2. [24]

However, even though Aaker can be credited with conceptualizing the idea of brand personality, I won't be recommending the specific approach shown in Figure 10.2. I'll explain why in a minute.

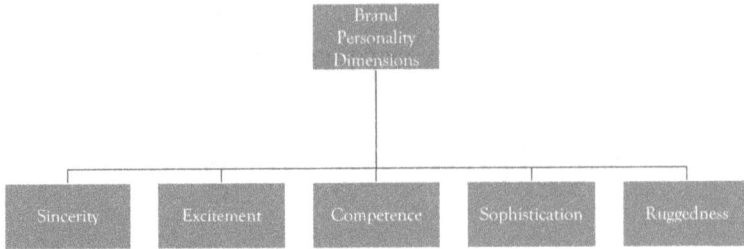

Figure 10.2 Brand personality dimensions

First, let's look at a couple of representative definitions of brand personality. Here's one offered by Brand Master Academy, which claims to be "The Training Ground For Brand Strategists":

Brand personality is **the collection of characteristics with which your brand is expressed in the market.** [25]
[Bold emphasis is in the source]

Interesting. Here's another definition, this one developed by Evan Tarver, writing at Investopedia.com. He says:

Brand personality is **a set of human characteristics that are attributed to a brand name [and]…should aim to elicit a positive emotional response from a targeted consumer segment.** [26]
[Bold emphasis added]

It's great to see these experts endorsing the importance of emotional connection, either directly or indirectly. However, it looks like they have missed a key point, one that I've discussed throughout this book. That is, that all aspects of branding, including the brand's personality, must be an outgrowth of its marketing position.

If you accept that as true—and I personally believe this to be true in every and all cases—then each and every brand's personality MUST be foundationally based on, and generated by, the brand's underlying marketing position.

Aaker's five dimensions don't refer to that fundamental truth. The definitions quoted previously don't overtly address the issue. In fact, standard definitions of brand personality don't speak directly to positioning's importance, if they acknowledge it at all.

In my view, the interconnection between the marketing position and the brand's personality—actually all aspects of branding—is something marketers ignore at their peril. As I've discussed, the entire market positioning process is a fully connected whole, from the first step to the last. The first step, your in-depth analysis, leads to the brand ladder; and that leads to your marketing position, which leads to developing an emotionally connected marketing strategy. And all that leads to the brand personality and every other aspect of branding, including your creative output—messaging, design, and all forms of creative execution.

There is an unalterable flow from step one through to each succeeding step, and it really can't be any other way.

***

As an alternative to the earlier definitions of brand personality, I'll offer the following. This version is predicated on the foundational, wholistic role of positioning:

Brand personality embodies and leverages the brand's marketing position by expressing specific human traits through messaging and stylistic/design elements to foster an emotional connection with the brand's intended audience—throughout the entire brand experience.

While this is wordier than I would like, it integrates valuable elements offered by leading brand personality experts, while also making clear both the centrality of market positioning and the vital role of emotion.

Importantly, this approach underscores that a brand's personality—indeed, the entire brand experience—simply cannot exist without the antecedent of an emotion-based marketing position for that brand.

***

It's worth a quick mention that many experts' definitions use the term "traits" instead of "characteristics," and others prefer "human characteristics." With that in mind, it's helpful to note that, just as human beings

have different personalities and traits—they can be charming or sophisticated or easy-going or obnoxious or unfriendly, among many, many other
possibilities—brands can also be described as having certain overall dis-
positions or identities.

***

In order to move ahead, let's accept my aforementioned brand personality definition as a workable option. With that as background, we can
take a look at the elements commonly employed when creating a brand
personality—although this is not intended to be a comprehensive list.

- **Messaging.** Written copy and design work together to
  effectively express a brand's marketing position—thus
  serving as the main components that shape that brand's
  personality. In my experience, starting with positioning-based,
  emotionally connected messaging/language almost always
  leads to the most resonant visual executions. Think of writing
  the lyrics for a song and then building the music around
  them.
- **Logo/logotype.** These are symbols, designs, or sometimes
  phrases intended to identify a product or company and set it
  clearly apart from competitors.
- **Color palette.** In advertising, a color palette or brand palette
  is a set of colors that work together in harmony and convey
  the emotion specifically identified in the emotional end
  benefit aspect of the positioning process.
- **Secondary typography.** This is the font (type style) that
  is used for everything other than the logo. That includes
  headlines, body copy, captions, package design, and so on.
  More than one font is often used in an individual brand's ads
  and communication; however, the number of fonts should
  be kept to a minimum and their characteristics should always
  align with the marketing position/emotional end benefit.
- **Page Architecture.** Page architecture is the hierarchical
  structure of your brochure layout, ad page(s), website page(s),
  and so on. Regarding your website, this architecture should

be structured so that visitors can easily find the information
they need while also helping search engines recognize the
relationship between different pages.
- **Imagery.** Imagery is a visual set of associations designed to
emotionally engage the consumer with the product. Images
can communicate more quickly and telegraphically than ad
copy (a picture is worth a thousand words).
- **Overall Visual Style.** Advertising and packaging create visual
style by using the seven visual elements of art: line, shape,
complex forms, texture, color, intensity, and space.

These various elements can be combined in an infinite number of
ways to communicate the marketing position to customers as the brand's
customer-facing brand personality.

In fact, when you do so with your brand, you will have completed
step five in the positioning process.

***

Having told you in broad terms how step five works, it's time to show
you with examples. But, rather than complicating things by trying to
delve into all of the elements from the previous list, let's isolate a single
one of the key components—visual imagery. By examining photos (these
are not actual ads) in a few recognizable categories, it will be enlighten-
ing to see how an individual factor can be used to express various brand
personalities.

For starters, everyone likes pictures of cars, don't they?

Automotive Images

The three images that follow all feature vehicles with four wheels and an
engine. And seats. In other words, cars. By exploring these generic types
of images—the visuals we see in car ads everywhere, all the time—we can
see how to apply the connection between a differentiating positioning and
a specific brand personality. Because, even though we'll be dealing with
pretty generic automobiles, in each case the imputed marketing position
does provide an opportunity for a well-differentiated presentation; in fact,

it turns out that the brand personalities of these products could hardly be more different.

Figure 10.3 Auto image 1

Source: Photo by Tyler Clemmensen on Unsplash.com.

What words would you use to describe this brand personality? Pleasant? Contemporary? Boring-striving-for-something-more?

The marketing position for many small-to-mid-size automotive sedans is "quality, reliability, and moderate price." Some cars in this category have recently started adding "sexy" styling changes that seem intended to attract a younger crowd, and there's a hint of that in this image, as well as a hint of adventure in the mountainous backdrop.

While the people featured in ads for this type of car tend to be young, they often are couples at the age when many are planning to start a family. Which makes sense—otherwise, why do they need a roomy sedan?

So, despite the fact that this car has a marginally racy design, the image is the very model of what is seen in many generic automotive lifestyle ads. Without a nameplate, you could literally insert most family sedans in its place—and whatever headline the writers come up with would probably still be applicable.

Figure 10.4 Auto image 2

Source: Photo by Reynier Carl on Unsplash.com.

Words to describe this image's brand personality could include adventurous and intrepid. Aspects of the image are also striving for "innovative and novel," although the vehicle itself, while certainly appearing to be adequate, doesn't support that part of the personality.

In terms of marketing position, if this were an ad, the position could be summed up as "rugged and ready for anything." And, again, while the vehicle in the photo appears to be a large, if run-of-the-mill, SUV, everything else about the image suggests daring, innovation, and a brash approach, flipping the normal relationship between auto and its driver and changing our expectations as a result. Because the driver is standing on the vehicle's roof (and is surrounded by rugged mountain peaks), we have the clear impression that he's an adventurer, and probably an out-of-the-box thinker who is happy to push the limits. In this context, it's interesting to note that the mountain backdrop and general setting are similar to the one in Figure 10.3, yet the feel is completely different.

The effect of the image therefore is to subtly transfer these "brand personality" qualities—daring, adventurous—to the unremarkable vehicle he's standing on. While the car looks like an ordinary SUV, the viewer is likely to think that it has bold, and even audacious, qualities.

Figure 10.5 Auto image 3

Source: Photo by Serjan Midili on Unsplash.com.

Words I'd use to describe this brand personality include: strong, aggressive, vigorous.

The abovementioned characteristics directly reflect the marketing position I would impute to this vehicle: a manly, potent, cutting-edge sportscar. This personality and positioning is emphasized by everything from the hard-edged, industrial-style setting to the way four men have gathered around the aggressively red vehicle and are apparently restlessly waiting their turn to slip behind the wheel and put the car through its paces. If this were executed as an ad, we could imagine an assertive headline in a bold typeface, with emphatic copy listing the car's many advanced attributes.

***

Looking at these three car images, we see widely varying approaches. Each can be viewed as embodying a specific, individual positioning while conveying a matching personality and sensibility to the relevant audience. But what would each ad actually be selling? Really not much more than transportation wrapped in different packaging.

It's also worth noting that all three images employ emotion in one way or another, although the emotional content is more of a subtle undercurrent in image #1. This suggests that, in differing ways, each image is attempting to make an emotional connection to its audience.

Retailer Images

Next, let's look at ads for "places to buy stuff at a discount"—three retail stores which, like the vehicles mentioned earlier, all have underlying similarities, yet portray dramatically different brand personalities.

Figure 10.6 Retailer image 1

Source: Photo by Xianjuan Hu on Unsplash.com.

Brand personality: Futuristic, highly organized, yet tacky.

This store shown here has a bifurcated marketing position: The initial impression is that it features high-tech products in a modern, well-lit, almost antiseptic, setting; and yet, a closer look shows that the merchandise is actually kitschy—the goods may be expensive, but that probably means they are overpriced. If this image were used in an ad for a retail outlet, it would be trying to leverage the clean, tech-y approach associated with Apple stores and other electronics shops. However, the merchandise here ranges from electric toothbrushes and make-up mirrors to plush dolls and various electronic toys, and may be of questionable quality.

Interestingly, the high-tech facade is subtly enhanced by the streaky image of a customer rushing through the frame—toward we don't know what. The implication of fast movement into the future belies the reality of the actual products for sale. The items may look futuristic at first glance, but they're likely to be found in a garage sale sooner than later.

Figure 10.7 Retailer image 2
Source: Photo by Bernard Hermant on Unsplash.com.

Brand personality: Overabundant, overwhelming, and overwhelmed.

Is there such a thing as too much abundance? Pity the poor store clerk who is apparently tasked with keeping track of all that inventory, which seems to continue endlessly in every direction. If this were an ad, it might be saying, "Come in and get crushed by too many choices!"

If that strikes you as breaking a major rule of market positioning ("Just one thing!"), you are correct. When an offering is trying to appeal as broadly as possible to its audience and strives (in this case almost oppressively) to meet every person's every possible need, then establishing a clear marketing position can be a challenge.

It's worth noting that this, in fact, is a capsule summary of the story of Sears, the former retail powerhouse. Known for many years as the place "where America shops," it diversified to such an extent that it was trying to be all things to everyone, selling everything from build-it-yourself kit houses to bicycles and baby diapers. When Sears lost its focus, it devolved into a shadow of the unstoppable marketing juggernaut it had once been.

Figure 10.8 Retailer image 3

Source: Photo by Kevin Turcios on Unsplash.com.

Brand personality: Stylish, trendy, and somewhat avant-garde.

Unlike the previous two retail images, this one appears to picture a small local shop, probably one that sells houseplants, among other items. And it conveys a very different attitude and personality than the previous retail images.

The positioning could, of course, be based on the store's unique attributes and differentiating features. However, the focus of the image is on the model in the foreground, and we can assume that her characteristics reflect the shop's personality, and therefore are an outgrowth of the marketing position. That extrapolation leads us to believe that the store is probably hip and fashionable. Maybe it sells exotic plants, or hand-crafted pots, for example.

In any case, if this image were used as the basis for an ad, it would deliver a significantly clearer, stronger, and more attractive marketing position than the prior retail examples.

***

As you can see, these three retail store images have vastly different brand personalities. And the marketing positions I've imputed vary dramatically, as would be expected.

Health Care Images

Now, let's change content dramatically and look at a few images focused on physicians. To state the obvious, the audience for ads using these types of images would be very different than the ones shown prior. While they would still be consumers, they would be looking for a brand personality that conveys reassurance, compassion, and expertise.

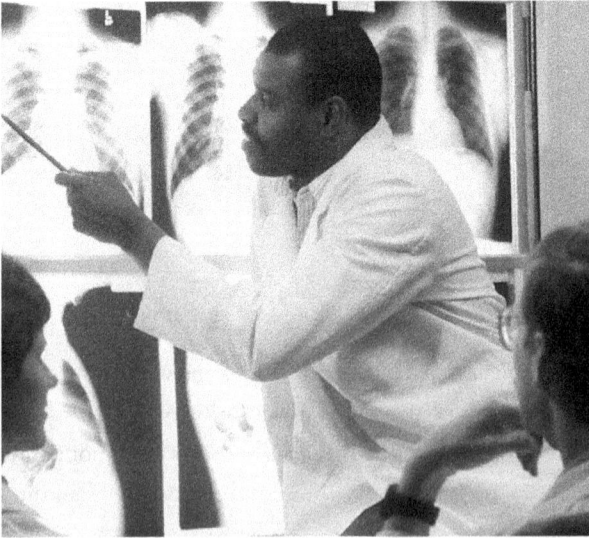

Figure 10.9 Health care image 1

Source: Photo by National Cancer Institute on Unsplash.com.

Brand personality: Intelligent, interested, scientific.

Physicians tend to think of themselves as scientists—a far cry from car buyers or retail shoppers—so if this image were to be used in an ad, it might be positioning the product (A radiology practice? A hospital? A medical teaching facility?) as demonstrating the scientific expertise of these affiliated doctors.

The setting in the image has the potential to be cold and impersonal, and the X-rays may indicate that serious medical conditions are being discussed. Yet the implication of a congenial, collegial, almost casual interaction within the medical team, and the level of interest they are showing, add some warmth. This leaves the viewer with a generally positive emotion.

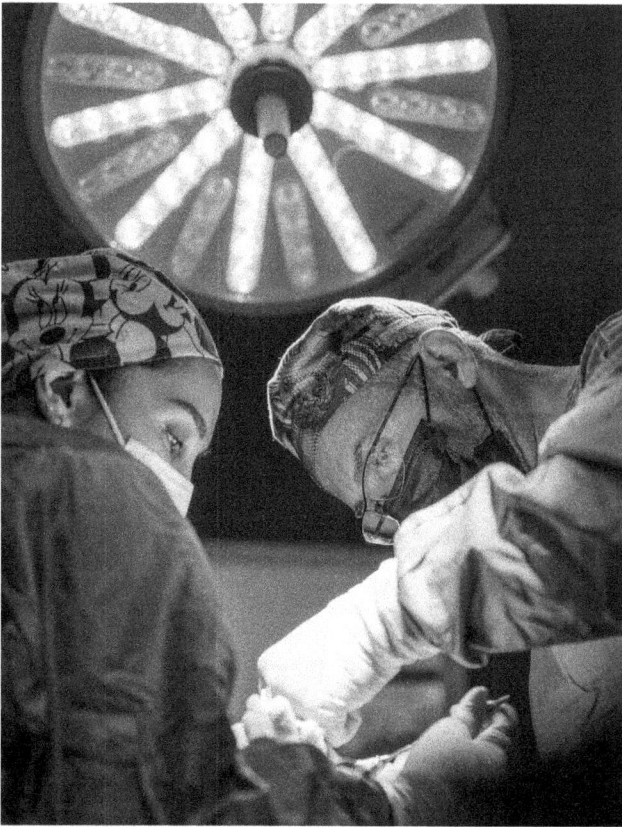

Figure 10.10 Health care image 2

Source: Photo by Akram Huseyn on Unsplash.com.

Brand personality: Professional, competent, yet compassionate.

This image is, in some ways, the flip side of the first one. While this again shows scientific expertise in action, witnessing a surgical procedure doesn't allow for much warmth or congeniality.

And yet, this too has emotional content. We have the sense that the situation could be a matter of life and death, and we get the feeling that the surgeon and his assistant are working in close, focused coordination. This adds an undercurrent of caring and urgency to what otherwise might be seen as a highly clinical situation.

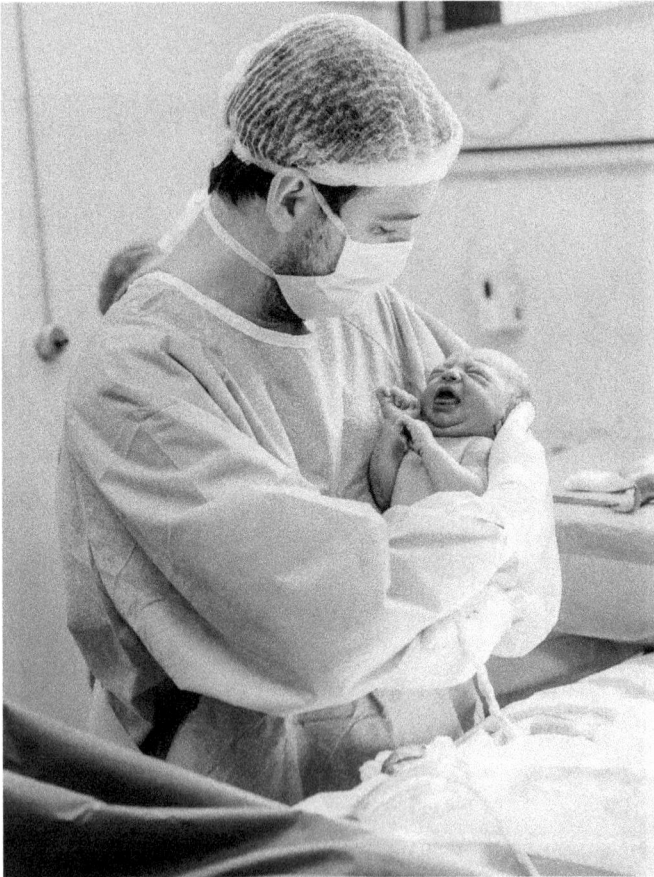

Figure 10.11 Health care image 3

Source: Photo by Jonathan Borba on Unsplash.com.

Brand personality: Caring, concerned, sensitive.

This image, while again portraying a clinical setting, is light years away from the first two. It's hard to determine if the man in the photo is a doctor or the baby's father but, in a way, it doesn't matter. Whoever he is, he appears to be completely, emotionally connected to the new life he holds in his arms.

Understandably, many, if not most, delivery room images focus on the mother, and/or some female medical personnel. This photo is differentiating not only because of the focus on a male figure, but also because of the obviously strong bond featured between the man and the child. If it were used in an ad for a hospital's maternity service, for example, it would have the opportunity to convey that kind of differentiation. It could suggest that the service's marketing position is that it goes out of its way to involve both genders in the birthing process.

***

Having reviewed these examples, what have we learned? First, it should be clear from this review that the logic and central thesis of this book are sound. In short, effective communication is based on a clear, focused brand personality; which, in turn, is an outgrowth of a solid marketing position. We can also see how important it is to make strong connections with the target audience on an emotional level.

> Brand personality, like all marketing activities, is an expression of your marketing position.

Reviewing the first two retail store photos depicted prior, we can also see how easily problems can occur when an offering's personality does not stem from a clear marketing position. In the case of those stores, the issue may be the formulation of the marketing position itself, or even more fundamentally, the base concept that resulted in the offering.

Here's what we can take away from these examples:

A rigorously followed positioning process generates the power that drives your brand's success.

Let me emphasize that. When you do the legwork to create a fully realized marketing position, and then leverage that work to effectively express your brand personality, your brand can be truly, fully brought to life.

And, by the way, when you do that, another extraordinary possibility can come tantalizingly into view. Because, when you give your brand the foundation of an enticing brand personality based on a solid marketing position, it then has the potential to live successfully in the marketplace for a potentially unlimited period of time. In short, it can become what I would call *a timeless brand*.

Let's review what this assertion is based on.

I'll start with this inescapable fact: When people develop a brand personality utilizing a vague, contradictory or broadly conceived positioning (refer back once more to the first two retail examples depicted earlier), they typically come up with a disjointed set of personality characteristics.

And, just like positioning needs to be a unified concept, so does a brand personality. Given that the branding follows directly from the unified marketing position in the first place, how could it be otherwise? And while it's not impossible for your brand personality to be effective if it features two or three different aspects, that will only work if those aspects are themselves fully and strategically aligned—and produce a coherent output as a result.

So the fact that Sears, for example, was able to avoid the pitfalls of an "all things for all people" marketing position for many, many decades is unusual, to say the least.

But let's try another, entirely generic example. A marketer, by following all of the preparatory steps, might have determined that dependability is a strong marketing position. Building on that foundation, she or he could decide to focus the brand's communication on dependability. And dependability can appropriately serve as a key personality characteristic for many types of products—think Toyota automobiles, Bosch kitchen appliances, and many medications.

However, instead of stopping there, let's consider a situation where the marketer gets carried away because the product also has aspects that can be considered innovative, or trendy, or compassionate, or a variety of other descriptors.

And it may be true that the brand does incorporate some, or even all of those other characteristics. If it does, you might well ask, why not include them in the brand personality? The problem is that there is no image, no typeface, no design, no logo, that can comfortably encompass and convey all of those things.

The idea of "dependability" will need a look that is solid, substantial, and upright. On the other hand, "innovation" might be shown by unique, out of the box images and designs that are intended to leap off the page or the screen and probably include bright, bold colors.

If you try to create a brand personality that integrates all of these aspects, you're giving your designers an impossible task. They will do their best, but the likely result will either be a messy mashup that doesn't convey anything of substance; or, out of desperation, your team may default to the kind of generic lifestyle depiction that is far too common in today's marketplace. If you watch television for five minutes, you've seen pharmaceutical ads filled with happily smiling, active people—and, remarkably, that look almost identical to dozens of other pharma ads. And this phenomenon is replicated well beyond the health care field.

It's essential to provide a brand personality description that your creative department *can actually use*. And that means it MUST be based on the product's singular marketing position. That's another of the foundational reasons that your positioning needs to be as solid and distinct as you can make it.

In every case.

And it's also why it needs to be formalized and finalized *before* you start developing the brand's personality. Only with the kind of solid foundation supplied by clear, differentiated positioning will you be enabled to identify a brand personality that is highly focused.

How highly focused should it be? The ideal brand personality will be based on *one word* that sums up its primary characteristic. If you absolutely need two or three characteristics, again, ensure they are fully and easily aligned. Examples of two aligned characteristics could be innovative and modern; three aligned aspects could be bold, strong, and determined.

With this type of focus, you won't be leaving any room for misinterpretation, or, at least, as little room as possible. The clearer you can be with your creative team (and, by extension, your audience), the more likely you are to present a brand personality that will be effective in the marketplace; and the more likely you are to have a brand that will come fully to life and thrive for its entire life cycle.

***

What Is a Timeless Brand?

In previous pages, we've mentioned Coca-Cola and Sears. These two companies were founded within a decade of each other at the end of the 1800s.

As of this writing, the Coca-Cola brand has dominated the soft drink market for more than 100 years, fending off competitors of all kinds. How successful are they today? For the 12 months ending September 30, 2022, Coca-Cola's revenue was $42.34 billion, a 12.01 percent increase year over year. [27]

On the other hand, there's Sears. For the better part of a century, the Sears brand dominated the American consumer market, first as a mail-order business and then in brick-and-mortar retail. But not anymore. Not for decades now.

So, what's the difference?

In a word, positioning.

Coca-Cola has maintained a consistent, distinct marketing position throughout its history. Sure, management tried to mess with it (more than once), but those misguided efforts didn't get very far.

Sears is another story. Sears ended up in such bad straits that it ended up being sold to Kmart. The reasons why are numerous, and there is plenty of blame to go around. As discussed earlier, a company that tries to be all things to all people, selling everything from furniture to automotive batteries to clothing and appliances, risks having a very unclear position in the marketplace.

That unclear position can open it up to aggressive, focused competition, and that's what Sears struggled to counter.

Looking at what befell Sears, it will be very interesting to look at Amazon in, say, 20, 50, or maybe 100 years. Aren't they, in many ways, the Sears of the 21st century? Just replace mail ordering with online ordering and the parallels seem clear. Not to mention the forays Amazon keeps making into brick-and-mortar retail.

If and when Amazon is faced with the kind of serious, determined competition that took down Sears, will they do a better job? Keep in mind what Jeffrey Wilke, Amazon's CEO of Worldwide Consumer said: "We don't want to distract ourselves from customers by obsessing over what competitors are doing or not doing."

Could that attitude lead to the same kind of mistakes Sears made?

There are factors in Amazon's favor. One, I believe, is the company's professed focus on going overboard to meet the needs of their customers—something that can't be said of Sears in recent decades. Also, Amazon has extraordinary digital capabilities to track and manage those customers as individuals' needs grow and change over time.

But an unwavering marketing position would certainly help, and they are so diverse and expansive, I'm not sure they have one that covers the territory.

It's also worth mentioning that Amazon's claimed focus on the customer appears to conflict with charges by the Federal Trade Commission that the company uses anticompetitive strategies to, among other things, degrade service for shoppers.

Could it be time for Amazon to do some additional positioning work?

***

Regardless of how things turn out for Amazon, it's reasonable to question if it will truly become what could be called a "timeless brand." On the other hand, it does actually feel like Coca-Cola can already be described that way.

Just think about it. Same taste. Same bottle. Same logo. **And essentially the same marketing position, for more than a century**.

A rarity indeed.

In the future, Coca-Cola will probably try new line extensions. Marketing campaigns will come and go. Strategies may be modified as the consumer world evolves.

But would it surprise you if, a couple of hundred years from now, the marketing position remained basically the same?

It wouldn't surprise me a bit.

Key Takeaways

- A brand's personality brings its marketing position fully to life.
- Messaging, design, and visuals are tools to express the brand's personality.
- A strong position can provide long-term security against the competition.

CHAPTER 11

Tactics, Campaigns, Branding Gaps...and the Secret to Success

Making sure your brand's position becomes the consistent foundation for all of your marketing activities can put you on the road to success.

By now, you've seen what a practical tool positioning can be. You've read that there's a specific sequence to the multistep positioning process, which is:

- Know your audience, in depth;
- Analyze your competitive environment;
- Determine your most differentiating, value-based, and emotionally impactful position in the marketplace, based on supportable reasons to believe;
- Center the emotion that will best create a positive connection with your audience;
- Identify and establish the brand personality that best expresses the previous steps.

At this point, you'll recognize that, *only after each of these sequential steps have been successfully accomplished*, is it time to think about marketing tactics—because those tactics, as well as the marketing campaigns that make use of them, must be based on and tied directly back to the product's marketing position.

To help you see how this works in practice, let's use a technique that could be called "branding gap discovery."

Here's how it works.

Start by getting your marketing position statement finalized and confirmed. If you're going to do the gap discovery exercise with a team, post that approved statement on a wall or whiteboard in letters readable from anywhere in the room. (NOTE: You can also use this "gap" technique on your own. In that case, simply attach the statement as a sticky note on the corner of your computer monitor.)

Your aim is to train everyone's attention and awareness on that bedrock positioning affirmation.

When I'm with a team, I make a show of reading the statement aloud, focusing on the reasons to believe, the Promise, and the emotional end benefit, and stressing how central positioning is to every marketing step they'll be taking going forward.

Also, with a team or without, I recommend briefly refreshing on your SWOT, your target audience and competitive analyses, and reviewing any other relevant project information.[1]

Next, display and explore the brand concepts currently in use by your primary competitors.

Let me explain what this means.

First, when I say display brand concepts, I'm talking about both messaging and visuals—although some marketers define a brand concept as the core idea behind the brand. In that case, you might express competitors' concepts solely as slogans, so visuals wouldn't be absolutely necessary. However, because many people are visually oriented, I've usually hung fully developed ads or campaign examples around the conference room when I've conducted gap exercises. I reveal that material only after going through the positioning statement and after any other preliminary discussion.

---

[1] Before beginning any tactical and creative work at all, and definitely before embarking on a full-blown campaign, your team will need to produce a document called a "creative brief" or "creative blueprint." This is a *summary of the project's essential information, including market and brand background, objectives, requirements, parameters, challenges, timeline,* and so on. The creative brief typically does not include any specific messaging language, visual images or design elements, though it sets the parameters and explains the characteristics of those elements, providing touchstones for the team when they are eventually created.

Second, the point of the exercise is to consider your competitors' brand concepts or campaigns in a continuum. So the material on the walls needs to be displayed in a range. For example, the continuum could range from lifestyle-based concepts or images on one end to iconic on the other; or from emotionally charged images to cold and impersonal ones; or from photographic to illustrated. There are of course many other possible ranges.

Whatever continuum you decide to use, your task then becomes identifying the gaps within that range.

To fully grasp what a gap means (and to better understand the process), let's start with the lifestyle-to-iconic spectrum. This is a very common range in advertising, regardless of the product or service. In the health care field, where I've spent many years, the strong tendency is to lean toward the lifestyle side of things. This is seen as a way to play it safe, which is an important consideration in health care marketing. And playing it safe is actually commonplace across the entire world of branding.

So let's take a quick look at the health care situation. A key reason the industry takes a very conservative approach is that the FDA's (entirely appropriate) regulatory rules and advertising restrictions encourage it. However, health care companies can take this careful mindset too far, and often do. The result is very cautious, sometimes mundane and "me-too" advertising and promotion—leaning far toward the lifestyle end of the spectrum. No doubt you've seen the countless medical ads featuring happy people engaged in pleasant, noncontroversial activities. These ads can be so similar they blend into each other.

So, while they may be presenting positive value, and making a mild emotional connection, these ads don't do very much in terms of differentiation.

But the truth is that, whatever industry you are in, staying within the bounds of conceptual safety doesn't have to result in undifferentiated output. Not at all. I frequently work with creative teams on health care concepts that are quite creative and even innovative, yet they remain comfortably within "safety" boundaries.

And it's not just me, of course. Those kinds of boundary-pushing options are routinely developed by creative agencies large and small, working in every type of industry. Unfortunately, in too many cases, those highly differentiating (and sometimes breathtaking) concepts are not the ones adopted by clients.

Getting back to the gap process, after you've displayed your competitors' materials around the room in a range, scan the walls. If you see that those opposing brands have congregated over on one side of the continuum—for example, by taking a safe, lifestyle approach—the need to differentiate your offering practically demands that you opt for something more unique and creative.

If you are willing to follow the principles of positioning—and if your creative team is willing to stretch itself—you might actually end up with something memorable, even iconic.

To put this in other words:

If you see any type of gap in the concepts your competitors are using, then fill it!

"Okay, that makes sense," you might say, "but what happens if filling the gap leads me toward 'iconic' concepts, but that approach conflicts with my brand's positioning and personality?"

This is a reasonable question, but it rarely happens in actual practice. However, if it does, I would always go back to the foundation of the brand's marketing—which means, of course, relying on the marketing position as your touchstone.

If your positioning is conservative, but you find the gap analysis pushing you toward iconic concepts, then it's correct and necessary to stay in the conservative lane. However, that still doesn't override the need for differentiation. So there's every good reason to be as creative as possible, within the boundaries of a careful and safe approach. And, the truth is, there is almost always a way to make that happen.

The Secret to Success

Is positioning the secret to success? Taken individually, the principles and practices presented in this book aren't much of a secret at all. Ries and Trout may have been the first to use positioning as a term, but marketers have undoubtedly made good use of positioning principles for as long as products and services have been sold. And while adding emotion as a central component of positioning expands the idea in a new direction, making emotional connections isn't new at all. Writers and artists dating at least from Aristophanes to Shakespeare and from Bularchus to Michelangelo—maybe as far back as the cave painters of Lascaux—intentionally used emotion to relate with their audiences and create a lasting connection.

In other words, in one form or another, these ideas have been around for a while. That's why it's kind of remarkable that none of the legends of marketing, whether it was Ries, Trout, Kotler, and Ogilvy, or Lauder, Disney, or Jobs, none of them ever developed a step-by-step, repeatable positioning process that marketing practitioners could apply in the marketplace. No one devised a system based on the three building blocks of positioning. No one codified the five steps of the positioning process into a structure that could serve as the basis for a brand's personality or that would functionally align promotional tactics and marketing campaigns that would reliably, consistently produce significant improvements in the bottom line.

It's reasonable to ask why.

As we've seen, even at this late date, no generally accepted definition of positioning exists. Perhaps, as Natasha Saqib has asserted, it's true that this lack of a clear definition has been a significant obstacle to operationalizing positioning.

Or maybe the problem is that the concept itself remains ambiguous. Again, here's Saqib: "...what exactly falls under the scope of positioning ...has not been sufficiently answered in literature and is still subject to heavy debate in the marketing community." [28]

Back when I took my first marketing post, when I was working with my mentor Larry Stern in the community relations department at Cherry Hill Medical Center, he insisted that I educate myself about "this positioning idea." Back then I knew little if anything about marketing, and less about basic marketing principles—I'd been a newspaper reporter less than a year earlier. So, when I started applying the concepts Larry was teaching me, I assumed that Ries and Trout had laid down the law, that there were well-accepted rules. I assumed that Larry and I were simply following those dictates.

But something unexpected happened.

It didn't take long for me to come up with insights of my own. I extrapolated from what Larry said, I interpreted what Ries and Trout had written. And, as time passed, bit by bit, through a lot of trial and some error, I developed a systematic process that bore real fruit. Over the years, I identified the three building blocks that produced powerful results for my clients and their offerings. And I used my systematic, five-step positioning process to great advantage.

And yet, when I became a consultant and talked about positioning with my clients—even many who were highly trained MBAs—three things became obvious. First, a surprising number weren't familiar with the positioning concept, and fewer had ever heard of Ries or Trout. Second, among those who were aware of the concept, many dismissed it as arcane or confusing.

But lastly, and most importantly, I realized that a key reason that people—including major corporations—weren't developing marketing positions was—they didn't know how. While I'd been learning about a variety of positioning formulas, many of which contained similar components, I couldn't seem to find a clear, repeatable system or process. It apparently didn't exist.

Kalafatis and his team honed in on this surprising reality when they wrote, "...[W]e have been unable to identify empirically developed and reliable positioning typologies and models that would allow the development of normative guidelines. . . . [There is a] paucity of coherent strategic positioning models." [29]

I believe that this longstanding lack of any formal, systematic, well-established, and generally accepted positioning process is a vacuum that has allowed, even encouraged, the ambiguity around positioning that continues to this day.

If this is, in fact, the reality, it can hardly be surprising that, when I recommend a systematic positioning process to my clients, I'm often—thankfully not always—faced with varying amounts of resistance. Many well-meaning and sincere clients say things like, "I'm sorry, but I don't have time for that kind of deep dive. What I need is marketing." Or, others say, "Y'know, that sounds like a lot of money. How about you just upgrade my website?"

I always carefully explain how important it is for such tasks to be grounded in a strong marketing position. But time and/or money are almost always limited; and, again, the concept remains at best opaque or, in some cases, entirely unknown to a surprising number of business people.

When a client asks me to "skip that stuff" and accomplish a specific task, I sometimes will agree—however, whenever possible, whenever practical, I perform a kind of stealth process (see the FSC example earlier in the book). For example, I might say, "Oh sure, that's fine, but how about we spend a couple of hours doing a quick SWOT analysis? It will pay bottom line dividends, I assure you." If they agree, I use the SWOT tool to get things started.

When I make use of such somewhat surreptitious methods, I hope it's clear that my intentions are honorable, my motivations ethical. I can say this with confidence because I've done the positioning process in enough situations to be totally convinced that *it will make my clients money.* They may not always be aware that positioning is happening in the background, but the results usually speak for themselves.

I'll admit that operating in a field that lacks real clarity has been, and continues to be, a challenge. If you've engaged in positioning work, you'll understand how difficult it can be to help clients succeed when the idea, the process, even the terminology you're using is obscure or, in many cases, totally foreign.

But we're marketers. *All we want is success. Every single time.*

This book is intended to help remedy the situation; to clarify the ambiguity that has persisted way too long. If the principles and process presented here can clear away the fog and guide people and businesses and organizations toward a strong marketing position, one that leads to powerful connections with their audiences—in other words, if I can help *you* succeed—then I will feel that I've made a genuine difference.

***

So, could it be that positioning is the secret to success after all? The following detailed case studies from my career demonstrate three ways that positioning does, indeed, deliver tremendous power.

Key Takeaways

- Your brand's marketing position must be the foundation for your marketing effort.
- Branding gap discovery can focus your positioning for tactics and campaigns.
- Positioning remains surprisingly obscure, yet is a key to marketing success.

CHAPTER 12

Illustrating Success

Detailed Case Studies

These case studies show positioning in action and illustrate how it can overcome the challenges and obstacles discussed in previous chapters.

Detailed Case Study #1: Positioning With Power Beats the Odds

As is detailed in the following, in 2004 the marketing team at AstraZeneca (AZ) approached Adient, a division of CommonHealth (now Ogilvy Health), seeking ways to boost their $1 billion/year Toprol-XL franchise. Toprol-XL (metoprolol succinate extended-release tablets) was one of the most successful blood pressure medications in the United States.

[NOTE: As of this writing, the product continues to be marketed under that brand name, although it is now sold by a different pharmaceutical manufacturer (see www.toprol-xl.com).]

Toprol-XL had already been on the U.S. market for more than a decade and was nearing the end of its patent life. It is extremely rare that pharmaceutical products are able to grow significantly at that stage in their life cycle. However, AZ tasked Adient with developing an initiative that would increase the product's annual bottom line by half a billion dollars.

Clearly, a significant challenge.

Our team at Adient increased the bottom line by even more—achieving ~$.7 billion growth.

The following is an edited and adapted version of Adient's written application for an internal CommonHealth company award. It was submitted in 2005 by Adient's management.

This statement makes clear the central role that identifying and leveraging Toprol-XL's positioning played in achieving the Adient team's remarkable success.

Nomination of the Toprol-XL Team at Adient for the 3rd Annual CommonGoal Award[1]

In early 2004, the Toprol-XL brand team at AstraZeneca and the marketing team at Adient agreed that, while AZ desired substantial growth for Toprol-XL, accomplishing such growth would be a significant challenge at this point in the product's life cycle. Yet the AZ brand team decided to charge Adient with meeting that challenge.

At that point, during an all-hands meeting, our team asked a simple question: "What is Toprol-XL's current marketing position?"

The response was that, even though the product had been on the market for a decade and had been highly successful, no rigorous positioning work had ever been conducted.

---

[1] **NOTE:** The CommonGoal Award was established in 2003 to annually honor those CommonHealth brand teams that best embodied the spirit of cooperation, respect, and strategic and tactical integration to which the agency's teams "should all aspire."

Criteria for nomination:

- Two or more CommonHealth companies must have collaborated together on marketing efforts for an existing client brand.
- Nominations must be sent accompanied by a brief, descriptive summary of the intercompany collaboration.
- Substantiation for the teams' efforts can include specific examples of extraordinary collaboration (e.g., joint development of integrated communications strategy), client feedback, business results, and so on.
- Creative samples, where appropriate, can accompany the submission.
- A list of all significant/core brand team members should also accompany the submission.
- The collaborative efforts must have occurred during the course of the past year.
- Nominations must be approved and signed by any one unit president of the cross-company brand team nominated.

The agency's Executive Committee reviewed all submissions, its votes were tallied, and The CommonGoal Award was given to the account team that was determined to best exhibit true *cross-company integration.*

Given this fact, our team recommended undertaking a highly focused market positioning research initiative. AZ management and staff soon authorized the Adient team to begin that work.

The results of that research effort were definitive. Almost without exception, the physicians we interviewed said that, even though AZ hadn't conducted a formal positioning process, Toprol-XL already had established a highly desirable brand position. Physicians' primary "reasons to believe" in the product were its inherent safety and the round-the-clock effectiveness of its once-daily dosing.

During the interviews, more than one physician used a version of the following phrase: "Toprol-XL is the beta blocker I believe in." Several physicians said that if their own parents ever needed a beta blocker, Toprol-XL would be their choice.

The research also confirmed that, while these excellent characteristics were inherently understood by many physicians, an overt marketing positioning had never been articulated or utilized in the company's marketing efforts. The potential benefits of a positioning process had never been maximized as a result. We believed that expressly communicating a clear marketing position to the prescribing physician audience offered a significant opportunity to increase product sales.

The Adient team documented these findings and submitted a formal market positioning and implementation process to AZ management for approval, which was quickly forthcoming.

After receiving approval, the team engaged in an organized positioning process, which included the development of viable reasons to believe and the identification of the product's emotional end benefit, the latter being phrased for internal communication purposes as "caring for the heart." Our team decided that the branding would visualize that emotional benefit and that the promotional message would be: "Toprol-XL: Trusted for consistent 24-hour coverage."

For 2004, AZ had established two key strategic drivers. The health care professional (HCP) driver was the acquisition of new prescriptions. For patients/consumers, the strategic driver was focused on patient persistence and adherence. It became clear that Adient's professional audience-oriented efforts could not operate in a silo. The codified position, branding, and resulting creative had to be "transferable" to patient promotion.

We addressed this aspect of the project by connecting to our colleagues at Quantum, the consumer promotion arm of CommonHealth. Meetings, conversations, and brainstorming with that team provided valuable insights into the mindset of the patient, their attitudes and behaviors regarding therapy, their persistence and adherence. Conversely, Adient's extensive experience in cardiovascular advertising and promotion aimed toward health care professionals gave Quantum valuable insights into the attitudes and prescribing behaviors of physicians, and their interactions with patients.

Adient proceeded with confidence, knowing that our marketing position and message was indeed "transferable" to patients. The lynchpin was the focus on "trust." HCPs consistently stated that they trusted Toprol-XL because of its 24-hour protection and coverage. Similarly, patients traditionally trust and rely on physicians' belief in the products they prescribe. With Toprol-XL, physicians' high comfort level with the product often translated into a similar comfort level for the patient.

[NOTE: Even today, "trust" is the primary message emphasized on the product's website.]

We discussed our findings with the client. They were pleased and impressed by our proactive collaborative efforts.

To some extent, this process anticipated CommonHealth's agencywide Collaborative Velocity effort—a cross-division approach to client servicing, which was introduced in the Fall of 2004. We became one of the first teams to make Collaborative Velocity a viable procedure for brand promotion at AstraZeneca.

From this point on, the Toprol-XL team was involved in a number of additional efforts involving the idea of Collaborative Velocity. The new branding needed to be extended into many promotional platforms and we began with the Toprol-XL website. Websites are, of course, among the most visible and accessible areas for brand promotion in health care. At the time, the website featured patient/consumer Heart Horizons branding instead of the product branding. The AZ brand team wanted this changed as quickly as possible.

We immediately began discussions with CommonHealth's digital division, Qi. With their help, we were able to analyze the overall product site in a comprehensive way, both consumer and HCP. We compiled extensive recommendations to address a variety of issues with the site. The client was pleased that we had leveraged the expertise of Qi to address the problems with the existing site.

Throughout 2004, our ability to use the resources of the entire CommonHealth network began to pay off measurably. There was a significant increase in the number of Toprol-XL projects for Adient—many above and beyond the approved workplan—and projects were assigned in areas where we had not previously been involved. We were awarded jobs in the managed care sector, e-promotion, medical education and the Azenity Service Force sector.

The Toprol-XL team at Adient had firmly established itself as a force for the coordination and management of all aspects of promotion. This may have helped to leverage Adient's strengths and creativity across to the relaunch of another AZ product, Atacand. It was a huge vote of confidence in Collaborative Velocity when Adient was appointed as the agency for the Atacand heart failure launch in early 2005. The brand team at AstraZeneca knew that there would be the same level of excellence and Collaborative Velocity on this important launch as there was on what had become their nearly $2 billion franchise of Toprol-XL.

Meanwhile, the Adient team identified an area of significant dissatisfaction at AZ: medical education efforts for Toprol-XL and Atacand, areas where CommonHealth had not been previously involved. We arranged for ProCom, the medical education division, to make a capabilities presentation to the AZ brand team for the 2005 operational plan. We met with ProCom and gave them a comprehensive overview of the history of Toprol-XL. We explained where the brand was going and the areas of focus they needed to address.

When the CommonGoal application was submitted, the brand team at AZ was undertaking an upsurge in direct-to-consumer (DTC) promotion. The Adient team had been intimately involved with Quantum for several months on DTC brand strategy and creative development, now in testing. Adient has worked hard to ensure that Quantum's work is aligned with appropriate strategic drivers, and that there is consistency in message and branding.

As our business grew, we understood the need for specialty promotions, specifically in managed markets. As Solara began to get involved at

AZ, we seized the opportunity. We worked hard to transition preexisting managed care projects to them, keeping true to Collaborative Velocity. Again, we have worked hard to ensure that Solara's work is aligned with appropriate strategic drivers, and that there is consistency in message and branding.

Overall in 2004, Adient's actual fee billing for Toprol-XL was almost double the original workplan. It is clear that, as our efforts in Collaborative Velocity grow, so does the business.

During 2004 and 2005, Adient has had multiple meetings/teleconferences with colleagues at Quantum (Direct to Patient/Consumer), Solara (Managed Markets Promotion), Xchange, ProCom, MBS/VOX (Physician/Patient Dialogue), Qi (Website and e-promotion), and Ferguson (Creative for Direct to Patient/Consumer).

In 2005, again, our actual fee billing for Toprol-XL for 2005 will exceed the original work plan. This is another endorsement of the Collaborative Velocity concept.

Based on the collaborative efforts of the Toprol-XL team at Adient described above, the significant growth of the core business for Toprol-XL, the spin-off growth of Atacand, potential Adient business for Toprolide-XL and Logimax, I would like to nominate the Toprol-XL team for the 3rd Annual CommonGoal Award.

Respectfully submitted,

Guy D. Dess

Detailed Case Study #2: Positioning a Community Church for Success

In 2018, the Orange Coast Unitarian Universalist Church in Costa Mesa, California, decided to develop and implement a marketing process. Church leadership learned that I had a marketing background and asked if I could help.

While I had worked in the nonprofit arena years earlier when I was marketing hospitals and a school district, marketing a church was a new and different type of challenge. To fully understand the nature of that challenge, it's important to provide the situation that most, if not all, religious organizations have been facing in recent years.

A situational overview was recently provided by the Gallup organization, as follows:

> Americans' membership in houses of worship continued to decline…dropping below 50 percent for the first time in Gallup's eight-decade trend. In 2020, 47 percent of Americans said they belonged to a church, synagogue or mosque, down from…70 percent in 1999.
>
> The decline in church membership is primarily a function of the increasing number of Americans who express no religious preference. Over the past two decades, the percentage of Americans who do not identify with any religion has grown from 8 percent in 1998–2000 to 13 percent in 2008–2010 and 21 percent over the past three years. [30]

The Orange Coast congregation is part of the Unitarian Universalist Association, which has historically been one of the smaller U.S. denominations. And, like most other U.S. denominations, overall Unitarian Universalist membership (as a percentage of the total U.S. population) has been slowly shrinking for the past 60 years. [31]

Any church—in any denomination—attempting to buck such a strong and nationwide negative trend would certainly be taking on an ambitious task. However, as a Unitarian Universalist church, Orange Coast faced additional challenges.

Unlike virtually every other significant U.S. denomination, Unitarian Universalists have no shared creed. Instead members share a covenant of principles that support "the free and responsible search for truth and meaning" [32]—in other words, Unitarian Universalists don't have a fixed set of beliefs. Members' backgrounds range from lapsed Catholics and Protestants to atheists, among many others.

While this diverse approach to belief is inclusive, coming up with an easily understood and brief summary and then finding a way to quickly convey it can make effective marketing difficult. In fact, over the years on a national basis, the Unitarian Universalist Association has implemented a number of marketing and advertising efforts, with little measurable effect.

The leaders of the Orange Coast church could be excused for wondering what could realistically be achieved in such an environment.

After several discussions, I recommended engaging in a positioning process, explaining that such a process could be designed to identify what differentiates Orange Coast—and, by extension, Unitarian Universalism—from other churches. They understood that this work would identify both advantages and disadvantages. Working together, we would use this process to discover the differentiating characteristic that delivers the greatest value to church members and the community, and also clarify how it provides that value.

Church leadership had long been convinced that the congregation contained something that made it special and distinct, what was referred to as a "nugget of meaning." All involved were aware that this nugget was hard to pin down or effectively describe.

After our discussions, they recognized that the positioning process had the potential to define this characteristic. They also soon came to understand that identifying the marketing position would ideally also serve as the basis for later decision making; that it would inform the organization's messaging to members and the public; and that it could also lay the groundwork for marketing tactics that might better connect the church to the community.

A volunteer task force was created and quickly got started.

As already discussed in Chapter 4 of this book, the first step in the process was to review any and all available data about the congregation and its characteristics, digging beneath the surface to uncover and analyze all relevant information.

The task force's primary data source was a congregational survey that had recently been conducted. Various interviews and anecdotal information were also explored.

When the analysis was complete, we engaged the members themselves in a democratic process to help narrow the learnings derived from the raw data. This involved distributing a list of congregational features and benefits that had surfaced during the analytical step, and asking members to rank them in terms of relevance and importance. This activity corresponds to the creation of a benefit ladder, as detailed in Chapter 5.

The results of that exercise became the basis we used to formulate the reasons to believe and the positioning statement for the church. While this was a challenging process, the task force soon developed a statement they all felt was a solid option.

At this point, the task force was asked the following questions:

- Does another church/congregation provide the value, as identified, to members or to the community at large better or more completely?
- Does the position statement need to be adjusted to make it more accurate?
- How comfortable would the congregation be with this position?
- Does this positioning statement fully and accurately match the congregation's essence?
- Does the statement leave room for future growth?
- Are we likely to need to revise the positioning statement in the near future?

After additional discussion, this positioning statement was finalized:

Orange Coast Unitarian Universalist Church is building a beloved, diverse community. We provide an authentic environment for all who seek spiritual and ethical development. Affirming, inclusive and open-minded, we nurture our individual spiritual paths and befriend one another as we go through life.

This is the marketing position approved by the congregation's board.

Following its adoption, the task force began developing overarching messages, with the objective of creating a single, lasting message that would become the "catchphrase" for the church. As discussed in Chapter 2, this message would be designed to reflect the sentiment of the position statement, but in a more public-facing way.

For this step, we reviewed a range of relevant sources, including:

- Recent messages implemented by Unitarian Universalist churches nationwide, and by the denomination as a whole;
- Messages being used by other churches and congregations;
- Messages from other types of relevant organizations.

The task force then generated its own ideas, thoughts, and phrases. Through this work, a set of six messages was developed that was then tested directly with church members. That testing was done by an e-mailed survey during March 2019. The results were tabulated and reviewed by the task force.

The highest scoring message, by far, was:

Many different beliefs, one loving community.

The task force then submitted this message to the board for approval, which was quickly forthcoming. The message has become the church's overarching theme. It headlines the website and is featured in a range of communications, worship services, and membership events.

Anecdotally, the marketing position and messaging appears to have encouraged a sense of cohesion and pride within the congregation. Also, reportedly, the church is increasingly attracting new members.

Detailed Case Study #3: Positioning as a Public Relations Technique

In 1989, relatively early in our careers, Ed Shankman and I, along with Cheryl Gaston, the head of the Gaston & Gordon agency, took on a significant challenge. At the time we were working in the public relations arena.

In those days, there was no World Wide Web. Social media did not exist. Yet, by employing the foundational principles of positioning and branding, we achieved a remarkable success. In fact, in the space of a few months, we transformed a mid-size American city's negative reaction about a tragic emergency response situation into positive public relations.

The following article appeared in the national publication, Public Relations News, *on September 4, 1989. It has been modified for this use.*

Few situations test the judgment and expertise of a strategist more than a community disaster. A carefully positioned, emotionally resonant and clear, candid, unified posture is essential when communicating with the public about this kind of difficult and demanding situation.

The tragic fire that took place 11 miles northwest of New York City on July 1, 1988 at an automobile dealership in Hackensack, New Jersey, resulted in the deaths of five city firefighters who were trapped in the back of the building. They were killed when the roof collapsed.

The tragedy threatened to bring down the entire city government of Hackensack because the public felt initially that casualties were the result of mismanagement. This perception was supported by inflammatory quotes and accusations from officials in the city government and a flood of negative letters to the area newspapers.

The public was told little about the blaze by city officials and firefighters. It was not until more than two months later that three separate agencies simultaneously released reports of the incident, one by a private investigator on behalf of the International Association of Firefighters; another by the National Fire Protection Association; and a third by the Bergen County (New Jersey) Prosecutor's Office.

The reports faulted the training, communications, and management of the Hackensack fire department. They cited "errors, misjudgment, and a lack of training" as factors directly responsible for the deaths of the five firefighters, a tragedy described by the media in such words as "preventable" and "needless."

The reaction to the three reports among the City Council, the fire department, and the firefighter's union was termed "unfocused anger," and the media carried hard-hitting recriminations. Fire Department officers, the City Council, the city manager, and the mayor were each answering queries from the media. When the media called, these officials reacted as individuals. There was no overall strategy for providing information to the press—and no real strategy of any kind.

As might be expected, the media and the public were harshly critical. There were numerous calls for the resignation of the fire chief and other fire department officers, as well as Hackensack's mayor. A crisis of confidence in both the fire department and city government reached perilous levels.

One month after the fire, a New Jersey public relations firm was retained by the city of Hackensack. According to the firm's vice president, Robert Gordon, the municipality's officials were not fully aware that a crisis situation was underway. They only asked Gordon and his team, which had previously worked on public relations for the Hackensack school system, to handle general press relations and to produce a newsletter similar to the one being done for the schools.

However, the situation quickly changed following release of the three reports and the unfavorable, angry outcry that resulted. It became evident that crisis PR approaches were essential.

Working with the PR company's owner, Cheryl Gaston, and its creative coordinator, Ed Shankman, Gordon organized a series of crisis meetings. Attending were the mayor, city manager, city council members, fire department officials, and the city attorney.

The attorney urged the officials to consider the potential legal ramifications of their statements and actions and strongly supported Gaston, Gordon, and Shankman's advice that communications in a crisis must be carefully controlled and strategically planned.

Given that key support, the team began a positioning and branding process. A comprehensive analysis of the situation was undertaken, data was gathered, and a marketing position was recommended. This focused on the city's history of good government and positive relations with the large majority of its residents and businesses. Based on this concept, the brand personality could have been summarized as reliable, effective, and caring.

It was strongly advised that only one qualified individual be authorized to speak for the city if the (until then) chaotic communications situation was to be resolved. As it happened, the abovementioned brand personality traits were characteristic of the city manager, Robert F. Casey. Gordon recommended that Casey become the face of the public response going forward.

Casey gained the support of the other city officials and assumed the critical sensitive communications role. An exclusive interview with *The Record*, Bergen county's largest newspaper, was arranged. This was followed by press conferences to which all New York metropolitan area news media were invited.

Then, on September 29, a statement from the mayor was widely distributed. The statement was entirely consistent with the communications coming from Casey and was intended to show solidarity among the city's top leadership.

It paid tribute to the "five heroic firefighters," and expressed compassion for their loss. In answer to recent accusations of inaction, the statement explained that, before anything could be done, it was necessary to wait for completion of the three official reports. The mayor then detailed the remedial steps that had been taken: establishment of a local fire scene communications channel; more aggressive fire inspections; and a mandatory advanced training program for all fire personnel. Subsequent interviews with Casey emphasized each of those positive steps, with all questions and answers handled by the city manager in consultation with Gordon and his team.

In early October, a unified communications policy began to show positive results. Letters to local newspapers indicated mitigation of earlier public anger and frustration. Fire fighter representatives expressed "cautious optimism" about the city's new approach to the emergency.

On November 9, the first favorable editorial appeared in northern New Jersey's daily newspaper, *The Record*. Headlined, "Good News in Hackensack," the editorial cited the efforts of Casey and fire department officials to make personnel changes for improving the department's leadership and lines of authority. The editorial concluded: "...it looks like an auspicious start in the effort to bolster Hackensack's fire department. For the first time since July, there's some good news for Hackensack firefighters."

Then, *The Record* ran a major article headlined, "State Backs Hackensack Fire Department." It noted that New Jersey fire officials investigating the disaster and the fire department's response to it found no "glaring problems" in the latter's actions. This was a major shift from the negative banner headlines the paper had run in the early days of the crisis.

Gordon said:

In our view, the willingness of the city manager and the mayor and council to present a consistent and positive position was the key element in the successful management of this crisis. Our advice was to point repeatedly and publicly to the positive actions being taken by the city and expose the public to detailed, positive information that clearly demonstrated a government that was in charge and effective. [33]

NOTE: Adapted from: *Public Relations News.* "How an Organization Turned Negative Reaction to an Emergency into Positive Public Response." Case Study No. 2187. September 4, 1989.

References

1. Ries A. and J. Trout. 1981. *Positioning: the Battle for Your Mind.* New York, NY: McGraw-Hill.
2. Bhat, S. and S.K. Reddy. 1998. "Symbolic and Functional Positioning of Brands." *Journal of Consumer Marketing* 15, no. 1, pp. 32–43.
3. Kotler, P. 2001. "New Forward to the Marketing Classic." In *Positioning: The Battle for Your Mind*, eds. A. Ries and J. Trout, p. ix. Revised ed. New York, NY: McGraw-Hill.
4. Kotler, P. 2001. "New Forward to the Marketing Classic." In *Positioning: The Battle for Your Mind*, eds. A. Ries and J. Trout, pp. ix–x. Revised ed. New York, NY: McGraw-Hill.
5. Kotler, P. 2001. "New Forward to the Marketing Classic." In *Positioning: The Battle for Your Mind*, eds. A. Ries and J. Trout, p. x. Revised ed. New York, NY: McGraw-Hill.
6. Kalafatis, S.P., M.H. Tsogas, and C. Blankson. 2000. "Positioning Strategies in Business Markets." *Journal of Business & Industrial Marketing* 15, no. 6, pp. 416–437.
7. Saqib, N. 2021. "Positioning–a Literature Review." *PSU Research Review* 5, no. 2, pp. 141–169.
8. Kalafatis, S.P., M.H. Tsogas, and C. Blankson. 2000. "Positioning Strategies in Business Markets." *Journal of Business & Industrial Marketing* 15, no. 6, pp. 416–437.
9. Saqib, N. 2021. "Positioning–a Literature Review." *PSU Research Review* 5, no. 2, pp. 141–169.
10. Dovel, G.P. 1990. "Stake It Out: Positioning Success, Step by Step." *Business Marketing* 5, pp. 43–51.
11. Ries, A. and J. Trout. 1981. *Positioning: the Battle for Your Mind.* New York, NY: McGraw-Hill.
12. Levitt, T. January 1980. "Marketing Success Through Differentiation—of Anything." *Harvard Business Review.* https://hbr.org/1980/01/marketing-success-through-differentiation-of-anything (accessed January 12, 2023).
13. Saitarli, V. April 2021. "More About Emotion, the Super Weapon of Marketing and Advertising." *Forbes Agency Council Post.*
14. Murray, P.N. February 2013. "How Emotions Influence What We Buy." *Psychology Today.* www.psychologytoday.com/us/blog/inside-the-consumer-mind/201302/how-emotions-influence-what-we-buy (accessed February 16, 2023).

15. Saitarli, V. November 2019. "Emotion: The Super Weapon of Marketing and Advertising." *Forbes Agency Council Post.*

16. Otamendi, F.J. and D.L. Sutil Martín. September 2020. "The Emotional Effectiveness of Advertisement." *Frontiers in Psychology* 11, pp. 1–12.

17. Business Makeover. January 27, 2023. "SWOT." https://businessmakeover .eu/tools/swot-.

18. Dalal, M. 2017. "Amazon Focused on Customers, Not Competitors: Jeffrey Wilke." *Livemint.com.* www.livemint.com/Companies/KEMppZz2Z DgiMLMshgQE6L/Amazon-focused-on-customers-not-competitors-Jeffrey-Wilke.html (accessed February 8, 2023).

19. Hattar, M. 2022. "Why Storytelling Wins in Marketing." *Forbes Communications Council Post.* www.forbes.com/sites/forbescommunicationscouncil /2022/06/09/why-storytelling-wins-in-marketing/?sh=40b2d95373a7 (accessed February 3, 2023).

20. Czerniawski, R. 2023. "Attribution Request." Email.

21. Trout, J. 1995. *The New Positioning.* New York, NY: McGraw-Hill.

22. Kotler, P. and K.L. Keller. 2009. *Marketing Management.* New York, NY: Pearson Education Inc.

23. Barry, B.W. 1998. *Strategic Planning Workbook for Nonprofit Organizations.* St. Paul, Minnesota: Amherst H. Wilder Foundation.

24. Aaker, J.L. 1997. "Dimensions of Brand Personality." *Journal of Marketing Research* 34, no. 3, pp. 347–356.

25. Brand Master Academy. 2021. "How to Develop a Brand Personality." https://brandmasteracademy.com/how-to-develop-brand-personality/ (accessed February 2, 2023).

26. Tarver, E. 2021. "What Is Brand Personality? How It Works and Examples." www.investopedia.com/terms/b/brand-personality.asp (accessed February 2, 2023).

27. www.macrotrends.net/stocks/charts/KO/cocacola/revenue#:~:text=CocaCola %20revenue%20for%20the%20quarter,increase%20year%2Dover%2Dyear (accessed February 8, 2023).

28. Saqib, N. 2021. "Positioning–a Literature Review." *PSU Research Review* 5, no. 2, pp. 141–169.

29. Kalafatis, S.P., M.H. Tsogas, and C. Blankson. 2000. "Positioning Strategies in Business Markets." *Journal of Business & Industrial Marketing* 15, no. 6, pp. 416–437.

30. Gallup. March 29, 2021. https://news.gallup.com/poll/341963/church-membership-falls-below-majority-first-time.aspx (accessed February 1, 2023).

31. Unitarian Universalist Association. 2023. "Aggregate Data From Unitarian Universalist Association Congregations. Membership Statistics, 1961–2020." www.uua.org/data/demographics/uua-statistics (accessed February 1, 2023).

32. Unitarian Universalist Association. 2023. "Beliefs & Principles." www.uua
.org/beliefs/what-we-believe (accessed February 2, 2023).
33. Case Study No. 2187. September 4, 1989. "How an Organization Turned
Negative Reaction to an Emergency Into Positive Public Response." [Adapted
from] *Public Relations News.*

About the Author

Robert S. (Rob) Gordon began his career as a journalist and, after being mentored by an expert health care marketer, moved quickly into hospital marketing and public relations. He has spent decades in advertising, marketing, and public relations with various agencies and organizations. Rob has provided marketing, promotion, and strategic communications expertise to organizations including Astra-Zeneca, J&J, and major hospitals and health care practices; and played a support role for Fortune 500 companies including ADP, BMW, Becton-Dickinson, and Humana. He has ghostwritten dozens of articles and provided a range of content for notable blogs, websites, and major publications. Rob has also worked with The Obesity Society, several start-up biotech companies, and a variety of small businesses.

Rob has applied positioning principles to everything from product and program launches and relaunches, to large-scale promotional and public relations campaigns, product naming, websites, video scripts, e-mail projects, sales aids, and print materials.

He played key roles on the teams that won a Silver Anvil Award from the Public Relations Society of America for a major environmental marketing campaign; the Sitecore Site of the Year for the development of websites for Humana; and the CommonGoal Award for a market positioning project of a billion-dollar blood pressure medication. He holds a master's degree in writing from Queens College of the City University of New York, and is the coauthor of the self-published novel, *The Backstage Man*.

Index

Note: Page numbers followed by "n" refer to foot notes.

OTHER TITLES IN THE MARKETING COLLECTION
Naresh Malhotra, Georgia Tech, Editor

- *Marketing of Consumer Financial Products* by Ritu Srivastava
- *The Big Miss* by Zhecho Dobrev
- *Digital Brand Romance* by Anna Harrison
- *Brand Vision* by James Everhart
- *Brand Naming* by Rob Meyerson
- *Fast Fulfillment* by Sanchoy Das
- *Multiply Your Business Value Through Brand & AI* by Rajan Narayan
- *Branding & AI* by Chahat Aggarwal
- *The Business Design Cube* by Rajagopal
- *Customer Relationship Management* by Michael Pearce
- *The Coming Age of Robots* by George Pettinico and George R. Milne
- *Market Entropy* by Rajagopal
- *Decoding Customer Value at the Bottom of the Pyramid* by Ritu Srivastava
- *Qualitative Marketing Research* by Rajagopal
- *Social Media Marketing* by Alan Charlesworth
- *Employee Ambassadorship* by Michael W Lowenstein

Concise and Applied Business Books

The Collection listed above is one of 30 business subject collections that Business Expert Press has grown to make BEP a premiere publisher of print and digital books. Our concise and applied books are for...

- Professionals and Practitioners
- Faculty who adopt our books for courses
- Librarians who know that BEP's Digital Libraries are a unique way to offer students ebooks to download, not restricted with any digital rights management
- Executive Training Course Leaders
- Business Seminar Organizers

Business Expert Press books are for anyone who needs to dig deeper on business ideas, goals, and solutions to everyday problems. Whether one print book, one ebook, or buying a digital library of 110 ebooks, we remain the affordable and smart way to be business smart. For more information, please visit www.businessexpertpress.com, or contact sales@businessexpertpress.com.

www.ingramcontent.com/pod-product-compliance
Lightning Source LLC
Chambersburg PA
CBHW061317220326
41599CB00026B/4925